D1104461

HOW TO
COPE WITH
LIFE TRANSITIONS

HOW TO COPE WITH LIFE TRANSITIONS: THE CHALLENGE OF PERSONAL CHANGE

Lawrence M. Brammer, Ph.D.
Professor Emeritus
University of Washington
Seattle, Washington

⬤HEMISPHERE PUBLISHING CORPORATION
A member of the Taylor & Francis Group
New York   Washington   Philadelphia   London

HOW TO COPE WITH LIFE TRANSITIONS: The Challenge of Personal Change

Copyright © 1991 by Hemisphere Publishing Corporation. All rights reserved. Printed in the United States of America. Except as permitted under the United States Copyright Act of 1976, no part of this publication may be reproduced or distributed in any form or by any means, or stored in a database or retrieval system, without the prior written permission of the publisher.

1 2 3 4 5 6 7 8 9 0   B R B R   9 8 7 6 5 4 3 2 1 0

This book was set in Times Roman by Hemisphere Publishing Corporation. The editors were Deanna D'Errico, John P. Rowan, and Deena Williams Newman; the managing editor was Ralph Eubanks; the production supervisor was Peggy M. Rote; and the typesetter was Phoebe Carter.
Cover design by Sharon M. DePass.
Printing and binding by Braun-Brumfield, Inc.

A CIP catalog record for this book is available from the British Library.

Library of Congress Cataloging-in-Publication Data

Brammer, Lawrence M.
    How to cope with life transitions: The challenge of personal
change / Lawrence M. Brammer.
        p.   cm.—(Series in death education, aging, and health care)
    Includes bibliographical references and index.
    1. Life change events—Psychological aspects.   2. Change
(Psychology)   3. Adjustment (Psychology)   I. Title.   II. Series.
BF637.L53B73   1990
155.9—dc20

ISBN 0-89116-962-8
ISSN 0275-3510

Contents

Preface

This is a book about personal change—ordinary change: birth, death, illness, marriage, divorce, unemployment, moves, job shifts, graduation, and promotion. It focuses especially on the short, sharp changes we call life transitions. The term life transitions means to journey through—usually to something unknown. This journey requires courage to take risks and to cope with fear. A key problem for people in the 1980s has been coping with rapid social, technological, and personal change. Trends cited by futurists indicate that the rate of this change will be even more rapid during the 1990s and will increase demands for skilled coping. What this means for us as individuals is escalating crises as we struggle to avoid obsolescence and manage the stress of faster change. Just as organizations need strategic plans to manage change, individuals need a strategic plan for coping with change.

Change often makes us anxious, but sometimes we are stimulated by it. In this book I emphasize two points: how we can cope with change comfortably and productively and how we can welcome change as an energizer and as a defense against boredom. Unproductive responses, however, exact a heavy price in anxiety, depression, illness, mistakes, and conflicts. Change strains our adaptive capacities and challenges us to develop more functional coping skills and attitudes.

This book is written primarily for the general reader who wants to understand and cope with the impact of change in his or her own life. It is written also for students who wish to learn about the nature of transitional change and how to mobilize their coping skills to manage change. The helping professional in counseling, teaching, nursing, medicine, social work, and psychology will find this book a useful source of ideas to describe to others what is happening in their transitions and how they might help them cope more effectively. Even though helping professionals are looking for new ways to explain the consequences of life changes to their clients, they will find that this book offers a personal checkup on the adequacy of their own coping skills and attitudes about change.

The data base for this book is primarily published research on coping and change. It is not possible, however, to cite all of the relevant studies and back all statements with citations. Much of the content is a distillation of a lifetime of readings and conferences on coping with change. Many ideas have come also from my 40 years of clinical experience with people in transition.

Examples of the kinds of life changes that are discussed in this book are changing relationships (such as divorce and death), termination of employment, disability and illness, and moving a residence. Positive changes, such as promotions, vacations, marriage, and parenting, also make demands on our coping skills. This book emphasizes general guidelines for managing these life transitions. Most self-help books focus on how to manage specific transitions, such as how to survive divorce, grieve over losses, cope with illness, change careers, or manage a midlife crisis. These topical books tend not to help the reader generalize to all life transitions, whereas this book stresses wide applicability of coping skills.

I wish to thank many people who helped with stimulating ideas and who, as students and colleagues, influenced me greatly. I am indebted to Drs. William Bridges, Barry Hopson, and Nancy Schlossberg for many ideas related to life transitions. I thank Father Herb Pins and Rev. Dr. Richard Bingea for their helpful suggestions from their long work with people in transition. I am especially grateful to Dr. Phil Abrego for ideas and illustrations developed together in earlier publications and workshops.

HOW TO
COPE WITH
LIFE TRANSITIONS

Chapter One

Change as Challenge and Opportunity

INTRODUCTION TO PERSONAL CHANGE

Don confided to a new acquaintance that the "bottom had just dropped out of his life." His self-confidence had plummeted. He felt helpless, depressed, angry, and afraid. Questioning revealed that he had just moved west to a new city, leaving friends and family behind. He had few job prospects, and he had just severed a significant relationship back home. The image of his life having no bottom was a realistic description; he was devastated by these multiple transitions. Don was fortunate, however, to have had successful coping experiences with previous transitions and an understanding listener in his new acquaintance. His initial job search uncovered several promising leads. In a few weeks he secured a good job and began making friends. With his effective coping skills and attitudes, Don was able to put a new bottom in his life.

Changes such as Don experienced strain our adaptive capacities. At the same time, these changes bring out hidden strengths in the form of coping resources we probably did not know existed. Don's reactions at first were pessimistic and self-defeating, but he viewed his new environment as a challenge and a test of his coping skills. Don's initial negative feelings were normal, even though this change was his choice. Self-initiated changes are stimulating, but usually they have some bad feelings associated with them also, as is illustrated in the following situations. Walter retired early with some anxious feelings that later were complicated with regrets. Herman felt depressed and vaguely ill while on an extended business trip. Georgina was baffled by her vague feelings of uneasiness and low energy on her long-awaited vacation to Hawaii. The Nelson family was bewildered by the complications of moving to a new community.

As distressing as self-initiated changes can be, they pale in comparison to the surprise transitions. Conrad was just informed of his wife's terminal illness. Al experienced much dread at his 40th birthday—a symbol of his declining physical capacities and growing obsolescence on his job. Peter was fired from his job of 20 years in a company reorganization. A widower talked about ending his life after his wife died. Susan developed a disabling cardiac condition. Jean was informed at dinner of her husband's plans for seeking a divorce. A family was devastated by a teenager's suicide. Kurt, a 50-year-old surgeon, lost a patient and was afraid that he was losing his skills and falling behind in essential technical knowledge. Allen experienced a disabling and disfiguring car accident. The Jones family lost everything they owned in a flash flood. This is just the beginning list of distressing common transitions in people's lives. These severe surprise changes do not include the ordinary, everyday hassles that pile up when the car will not start, the keys are lost, no change can be found for the parking meter, the children are crying, and a police officer stops you.

Reactions to these common events are complicated by rapid social changes. We are bombarded daily in the mass media about mysterious technical advances, distressing world conflicts, massive political changes, and agonizing terrorism. In addition, almost every occupation is undergoing rapid change. Physicians, engineers, teachers, and business managers, for example, face constant technological change that makes them angry and fearful. This "transition anxiety" is the nagging fear that one cannot keep up and that one is in great danger of forced obsolescence. Organizations are changing in structure and function, sometimes so rapidly that transition shock is experienced by the long-tenured employees. For example, Ward estimated that more than half of the Fortune 1000 companies experienced significant reorganization in the 1980s.[1] In 1988 more than 4,000 companies were engaged in a massive organizational face lift.

SPECIAL GROUPS IN TRANSITION

The problems of coping with life transitions are even more complex for special groups. For example, the effects of separation or divorce on women with small children and the impact of unemployment or dropping out of school on Black teenagers are overpowering. In a pluralistic society such as America, there are many diverse ethnic and minority groups that have unique ideas about what is helpful or healing. Differences in people's backgrounds must be recognized and respected.

Space is limited for discussing many of these special problem situations, but I feel compelled to mention the special problems of young mothers separated from their husbands. Not only must they work through the traumatic transition, but also they often must cope with rearing children under poverty conditions. At the same time, they must prepare for reentry into the paid employment world, because alimony and child support arrangements usually are not sufficient for their long-term needs. In addition to financial resources, these women need extraordinary coping skills to survive their multiple transitions.

Minority groups often face similar transitional difficulties. For example, if the single mother is black, her problems are even more complex. If the person is a minority teenager who is in the transition from school to work, the problems of employment or reemployment put great strain on coping capacity and morale. In addition, a minority youth whose employment is terminated or who is released from military service or the criminal justice system must overcome enormous obstacles to further education and reemployment. The poverty stricken of any race or ethnic background face the usual adjustment problems to a system with which they are disillusioned. Transitional changes compound their difficult adjustments. Low-income, homeless, and disabled people also need extraordinary coping skills, as well as expanded opportunities for education and jobs, to supplement their street smart survival skills.

This book will help you to cope with the cumulative stressful impact of such broad social and organizational changes. The plan of this book is to consider your transitions as follows:

• Describe how people view life transitions, and particularly how you view and manage your transitions.
• Describe the stages of reacting to a transition and suggest ways of managing the change process at critical points.
• Present specific coping skills and strategies for managing life transitions.
• Apply the general principles and skills to specific transitions and describe how these transitions lead to renewal and growth.

This chapter takes you through personal reactions to change, how you can view the main transitions of your lifetime, and how you can make sense out of your present or anticipated transitions.

HOW DO YOU REACT TO CHANGE?

The Definition of Transition

In the Preface I gave a brief definition of *transition* that was stated originally by Hopson and Adams, namely that transitions are characterized by a sharp discontinuity with previous life events and emergence of coping responses that the person often did not know that he or she had.[2] Transitions usually are short-term events, but time is experienced usually as slow-moving, almost dragging. The term *transition* has other meanings also, such as the brief and unstable period between human developmental stages. For example, the transition from childhood to adolescence usually lasts a year or two, and it is often an unsettled period during which the person moves through profound physical and emotional changes.

A third meaning of *transition* used currently is the period between broad social eras. Our present time, for example, may be described as a transition period between the industrial and informational eras. This book focuses on the first of these meanings—namely, a short time of personal change with a definite beginning and ending.

Personal Reactions to Transitions

Recall an event that changed your life profoundly. What were your thoughts and feelings at that time? Your thoughts triggered by this event very likely were centered on how this change was going to affect your life. This is true especially if this event involved a loss, such as a job termination or failure in school.

Keep in mind that even a positive event, such as receiving a college degree or a job promotion, can cause anxiety and is likely to be experienced as a loss. An example is George, who was promoted to assistant manager but saw this event as a loss of his friends because of a now different social status. Nonevents, such as not receiving a promotion that was expected, can have the same effect as loss. It may seem strange, but unpleasant events often have positive outcomes. An example is loss of a parent who was receiving total care from a daughter, who also experienced great relief from the demanding caregiving tasks. In any case, these kinds of events and nonevents set off thoughtful speculation and deep feelings of loss.

What was your emotional reaction to this change in your life? It probably was a mixture of fear, guilt, resentment, and pleasure. The dominant feeling depended on the type of event. Keep the event in the foreground of your awareness for a while, and relate it to the following ideas and activities.

Change as Loss and Grief

The experience of loss puts us into a mourning process that we feel as grief. We trust, however, that this grieving process will mobilize our coping resources and will lead to healing and renewal. It is reassuring to know that renewal usually takes place in due time. Recovery, sometimes called the *circle of healing*, follows this sequence of experiences:

- The change event shakes us. Stability and continuity with the past is broken.
- Change is experienced as loss. Life routines are disrupted painfully.
- Loss precipitates mourning. Feelings of grief are experienced.
- Coping skills and attitudes are mobilized. Life again becomes manageable.
- Healing processes proceed. The hold on the past is released.
- Renewal takes place. New goals are set and tried.
- Growth continues. Changes are viewed as more manageable, sometimes challenging, life events.

This relation between grief and loss is obvious in the case of severe loss. It is not easy, however, to see how events such as vacations or promotions could be experienced as losses. Yet, when we take a vacation trip we give up our comfortable surroundings—bed, language, and people—and are forced to make adaptations. Not only is this process exhausting, but also we often feel sad and uneasy, even depressed. Sometimes we say, how can this be? A vacation is supposed to be a happy time, a period of renewal. But when we reflect on the changes that we experience on a vacation trip, this mourning response is more understandable.

Similarly, a promotion means leaving old friends and haunts, especially if it involves movement from worker to manager, or from enlisted person to officer in the military. We go through a process of giving up the old and familiar for the new and untried. We do not know the special responses required in the new job, for example, and we fear the anticipated rejection or criticism of our new co-workers. Take a few minutes now to review the losses and gains of your current or recent transition. Retain your list for later application activities.

The greatest lesson to be learned from our life changes is that successful management of transitional change requires giving up on old value, behavior, or relationship and taking hold of a new one. For example, if a friend leaves us, we must let go of that relationship emotionally so that new friendships can be made. This does not mean that we forget the friend or that we do not grieve for him or her. How we accomplish this process of letting go and taking hold is covered in the next chapter.

VIEWING CHANGE AS A FRIENDLY EVENT

When going through the pain of a transition and viewing the change adversely, it is difficult to see the benefits such a change may hold for us. As the healing process progresses, however, we begin to see how this change was a great challenge to our coping skills, how the event forced a fresh start, or how the process provoked a long overdue self-assessment and redirection. Thus, change could be the most life-giving event that one could experience. A client once said to me after he was dismissed permanently from his job, "I saw this coming; they did me a favor [to fire me]. Now I want to do something more satisfying and productive."

Viewing Change as a Challenge

One of the most effective coping attitudes, which is confirmed by Kobassa's research on coping, is to view change as a welcome challenge.[3] This means that we view the transition as an opportunity to solve a difficult problem, and that we learn more about ourselves from the way we managed this change event. Effective copers welcome change as a stimulus for growth or as a means of escaping a comfortable rut. We seek challenges such as developing new careers, climbing mountains, or writing books because of the exhilaration and renewed energy that accompany such changes. These fresh tasks take us out of the stultifying and frustrating routines of living and open new possibilities for growth. George, for example, saw his company reorganization as a threat to his continued employment. He decided to use this experience as a reason to move to a career he always wanted: a business of his own. He viewed this move as a challenging opportunity.

Viewing Change as an Opportunity for Creative Growth

A self-initiated transition can be the trigger for an explosive creative experience. Seeking stimulation is the basis for a four-step creative approach to coping with change:

1 Disruption
2 Incubation
3 Transformation
4 Action

Disruption   Creativity demands that an experience (such as a life transition) disrupt our behavior and reorient our thinking. The first step is to alter our previous behavior and levels of comfort. This action allows new possibilities for thinking and acting to emerge. Transitions naturally provide this disruption process. Vacations, hobbies, and professional leaves are examples of self-chosen and controlled disruptions.

Incubation   The second step in our response to change is an incubation period when ideas quietly simmer, or bubble and boil if the change is abrupt. It often is an uncomfortable experience, because our openness to new ideas and attempts to be flexible in our actions make us anxious. Yet, we also must detach ourselves from our comfortable routines. As you will note in the next chapter, this period of detachment and reflection in managing transitions offers a great opportunity to consider new directions, relationships, and values for your life. We do this through planned quiet time, meditation and relaxation, or recreational activities.

Transformation Detachment and contemplation ready us for the third step in this creative growth process: transformation. This is an insightful or "ah ha" experience, when new ideas tumble over one another, and the world is seen differently. This is the critical point when we are ready to grasp a new way of thinking or acting. This change is facilitated when we deliberately attempt to give up or let go of the past routines, ideas, people, or situations that have been inhibiting change. How this transformational change takes place is discussed later.

Action Awareness of new possibilities for our lives motivates us to take the fourth creative step: to put our new ideas into practice. We actively seek the new partner or job, for example. This final stage of letting go and taking hold involves setting new goals and making new plans. When the implementation step in this creative process is under way, you will find that your mood tends to change from discouragement, sadness, and fear to optimism, hope, and joy. Smiles and energy reappear. Everyday tasks appear easier.

Viewing Change as Being Normal

Viewing changes in life as a normal part of living goes far in helping people cope with the strain of those changes. If one looks at a transitional change as a terrible problem to solve, or curse it as an unlucky event, distress continues. Effective copers look upon life changes as normal occurrences that must be taken in stride. What is your view of transitions? Are they detestable intrusions into your stable life, or do you view them as events to be accepted as part of life and thus to be managed as effectively as possible? If your view of change is a problem for you, the techniques for changing such thoughts and perceptions described in chapter 4 would be relevant.

RESPONSES TO CHANGE

One goal for managing life transitions effectively is to choose the appropriate level of response to those changes. Figure 1-1 shows some options, with the most automatic and easiest forms at the bottom and the most elusive and difficult toward the top.

Adjustment

Adjustment is an automatic adaptational response to environmental pressure. For example, one of the lowest organisms in the animal chain is the parame-

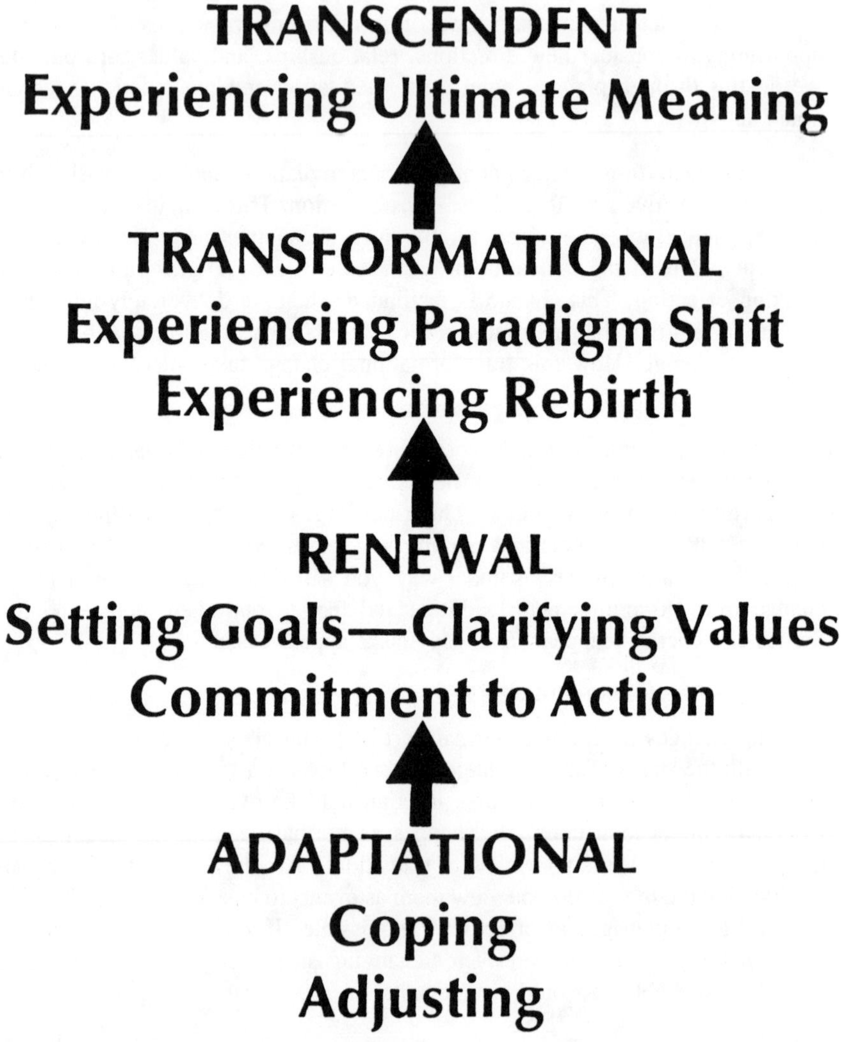

TRANSCENDENT
Experiencing Ultimate Meaning

↑

TRANSFORMATIONAL
Experiencing Paradigm Shift
Experiencing Rebirth

↑

RENEWAL
Setting Goals—Clarifying Values
Commitment to Action

↑

ADAPTATIONAL
Coping
Adjusting

Figure 1-1 Modes of responding to change.

cium. Its adjustment is masterly as it slithers through fluid, reshaping itself to correspond to pressures from obstacles or contacts with other forms of life. Similarly, we sometimes appraise a life change as one to which we choose to adjust. Adjusting to the situation may be the prudent thing to do when the consequences are not important to us or when it is futile to resist. When we get a traffic ticket, for example, we may decide to accept the ticket without comment and pay the fine without protest.

Coping

We may also decide to use a coping response, which is a more active problem-solving approach to adaptation. Before coping, we question, appraise danger, set goals, and choose among alternatives to action. Coping strategies include some basic attitudes and skills, such as

- developing a positive view of change (opportunity, control, and responsibility);
- building support (professional networks, family, and friends);
- changing negative thoughts;
- managing stress constructively;
- solving problems; and
- appraising potential danger.

Although there are several ways of classifying coping skills, I have found this list to be the most clear and understandable. Later chapters describe these coping skills and suggest practical applications.

There is a growing body of research on coping—notably that of Lazarus and Folkman.[4] A key idea from this research in coping is that the person faced with a change, threat, or a crisis first *appraises* the degree of danger. Effective copers have thought processes that enable them to appraise a change event accurately to discover potential danger. There are four appraisal responses to the question, "Is this change dangerous?"

- Decide that the threat is indeed dangerous and that I must take defensive steps immediately, such as flight or fight.
- Decide that the threatening event is benign, or not dangerous; hence, I choose not to act.
- Decide that the event is mainly annoying, and so I choose to avoid or ignore it if possible.
- Decide that this change is a challenge to my growth, so I choose effective coping responses.

Animals depend on the first two options of this basic appraisal process as a survival strategy. The goal of humans is to sharpen our appraisal and coping skills so that we can prepare for action only when necessary. Then, in dangerous situations, we can choose the most appropriate response to the threatening change event. Thus, we do not need to depend on automatic, massive mobilization of basic defense mechanisms for survival.

Three basic assumptions underlying coping are

1 We have a vast reservoir of unused capacity to cope with life changes in productive ways.
2 We can learn more effective coping skills and attitudes.
3 We can grow from the challenge to cope constructively and creatively.

Renewal

This change strategy is a deliberate effort to direct change in a creative personal direction. As the word implies, it is a process of making new again. We can initiate a renewal process most appropriately when we are not trying to cope with an involuntary transitional change. In other words, we may seek change in the renewal mode when life becomes dull, unchallenging, and enervating. People who deliberately make stressful choices, such as risky finance ventures or mountain climbing, often are seeking renewal.

Taking risks is a very personal decision. We vary from one another in our willingness to take risks. Of course, I am not speaking of life-threatening or foolhardy types of risks, but rather, psychological risks that may cause us to be vulnerable to feelings of failure, criticism from others, or ridicule. Risking means accepting the possibility of failure. Renewal involves setting new goals and planning new directions for our lives, which means reaching out into the unknown at times. This can be risky, but this very sense of risk adds zest to the activity. Some examples of taking risks are changing from a comfortable but unchallenging job to one with high demands and possibility for failure, deciding to take up skydiving in middle age, competing for professional school admission, or marrying a person of a different race or religion.

Transformation

A transformational change is a basic shift in the way a problem or situation is viewed. For example, you might look at a transition as a great tragedy and that you will suffer with it for a long time. You might transform or reframe the meaning of this transition as an unhappy event, to a keen challenge or an intriguing problem. Transformational change also refers to broader value shifts such as looking at unplanned life events not as tragedies but as valued opportunities to learn about one's self, the world, and the process of change. This shift of thinking is a coping response that can be learned.

Transcendence

In this form of change you experience ultimate meanings of life. Transcendence is a difficult state to achieve directly, because it usually is a by-product of other experiences such as reflection, suffering, or work. It is the culmination of a search for meaning in the transition, but usually it does not come as a result of an active intellectual process. It comes rather as a sweeping awareness of the meaning of this transition, or even the meaning of one's whole life. This change of meaning is usually sudden and unexpected. Occasionally, this change is accompanied by feelings of joy and peace.

Some religious enlightenment or conversion experiences fall into the transcendent category of change. Zen novices in the Buddhist tradition, for example, aim for *satori*—a high level of awareness or enlightenment that results in transcendental change of meaning. It may emerge at odd times, such as when washing dishes or chopping wood. Although this form of personal change is a desirable outcome of a transition, it is highly unlikely to take place in ordinary life transitions without further experiences. If it should happen to you, however, it would be a fantastic bonus!

TRANSITIONS AS EVENTS ON YOUR LIFELINE

People think of their lives with visual images such as a lifeline, or a circle, with the key transitions plotted in sequence. In Western cultures a horizontal line is a common image because we tend to view life as a continuous line of time between birth and death. In other cultures, particularly the Eastern, life is perceived as more cyclic and proceeds like a spiral; thus, events tend to repeat, implying that if this opportunity is not grasped another will come along in due time. Recall of earlier transitions also helps to understand present transitions. Mark, for example, saw how his response to an earlier car accident paralleled his responses to his present transition from failure in college and return to the work force. In this section I suggest ways of gaining awareness of your life events—by examining images, dreams, and feelings and reflecting on the meaning of them. Then I demonstrate how you can use this information to plot your own lifeline.

Awareness of Images

Think about your life transitions, be open to images that appear in your awareness, and record them as they appear. These images, or metaphors, are as old as human beings. Some images become so commonplace that writers such as Jung[5] built much of their theory of personality and counseling around them. Jung called these basic human images archetypes those primitive symbols that come from the accumulated history of the human race. Examples are nurturant mothers, difficult journeys, humanized animals, and wise old men.

Classical literature is full of references to basic human images. The journey of life is one of these. Throughout history people searched for something grand—the Holy Grail, the meaning of life, a religious relic. Homer's epic poem about Odysseus's trip to Troy and back that took more than 10 years is an example. Bridges traced the meanings of this journey and pointed out also that in literature the heroes in these epics were men.[6] Modern literature reflects more feminine images and heroines such that women also can find personal meaning in them.

Campbell pointed out that these trips from classical literature and the prehistoric stories had a hero who heeded the call to adventure and went through a series of transitions.[7] The heroes usually left alone on a magnificent quest and faced many trials and challenges in the pursuit of their goals. Finally, the hero returned after a lengthy and demanding journey. He usually came home a transformed person as a result of suffering and overcoming successive obstacles. Although your image of a life journey may not be as detailed as an epic poem, it could have many parallels. It is important to write these down if the image of your lifeline emerges as lengthy and stressful journey, for example.

Other modern images that come to awareness are mechanical objects such as fast sports cars or a powerful truck. Men often refer to their bodies as "machines." This symbol implies that after they are constructed they need considerable maintenance, they wear out or become obsolete, and finally they are junked. Some people think in natural images around plant cycles, phases of the moon, seasons of the year, or degrees of lightness and darkness. American frontier heroes with their images of rugged independence and bravado sometimes emerge. Chapters in a novel, a biography, or a short life story often are productive images of our lives. Animals also are prominent images. Ask yourself, "If my workplace were a zoo, what animal would I be?" What does it mean, for example, if you see yourself as a workhorse, a mouse, a snake, or a cheetah? What characteristics do you have in common?

Many women with traditional experiences tended to have images of life's continuity such as cycles of birth and death and rituals around housekeeping. Home was the symbol of and the center of her universe. The modern woman, however, needs more updated images and metaphors that reflect her complex roles of employee, parent, wife, home manager, and community worker. If this is your situation, what descriptive images fit you?

Awareness of Dreams and Feelings

Interpreting the content of dreams is another route to awareness. Dreams, of course, are heavily shrouded in symbolism and take much study and expertise to interpret. Even then, the meaning is only suggestive. In the final analysis, each of us must interpret his or her own dreams. Record your dreams and fragments as soon as you awaken. Look at the patterns and let the meanings emerge. Compare them with your daydreams and life events.

As you trace your transitions and record the images and dreams from your flow of life, be aware of your feelings as you experience this task. You will find that a wide range of anxiety, anger, and guilt will sweep over you as you proceed through this task. Tag ends of unresolved grief are likely to reappear, so be prepared to experience old feelings again. Record these feelings as soon as possible for later reflection and interpretation.

Reflection

After you have made yourself aware of the images, dreams, and feelings associated with your life transitions, reflect on their meaning. Let them tumble around in your thoughts when you are in a relaxed state. Additional meanings are likely to come with a minimum of direct effort. Discuss them with a trusted relative or friend in your support network. It is better to discuss these findings with a friend who has had similar experiences in recording his or her lifeline. In workshop settings, such personal discussions take place as a natural part of the learning experience. Discussing your thoughts and feelings about your life transitions with others helps to clarify and amplify your ideas. Note the patterns and consistencies. For example, you might see patterns of defeat and powerlessness, of strength in adversity, or of isolation and retreat. Additional advantages of group discussions are that they help you resolve feelings about a transition that have not reached closure, and they assure you of the normality of your experiences. If this lifeline review experience turns out to be painful because it persistently brings up old feelings, it would help to share them with a trusted friend. Additional images and feelings will appear often as you discuss your lifeline. Add these feelings to your list.

Application Activity: Plotting Your Lifeline

In the foregoing paragraphs, you were shown how to use imagery, dreams, feelings, and reflections to gain awareness of what your main transitions were and how you felt about them. One meaningful way of expressing the events of your life visually is to plot a lifeline, such as the one depicted in Figure 1-2. The vertical dimension is self-esteem and mood, with the lifeline entry as the middle or stable point of reference. The horizontal dimension is time. You will note in this example that going off to school was a short but pleasant event. Getting married was pleasurable, too, whereas getting divorced shortly afterward was a sad transition for this person. As you trace your lifeline to the

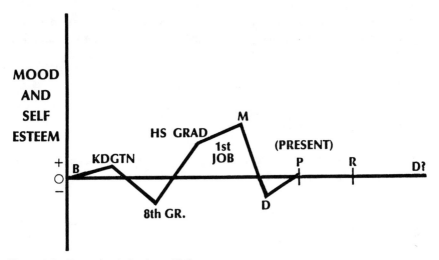

Figure 1-2 Example of plotting a lifeline.

present, use symbols and events that are meaningful to you. You might find it productive also to plot some anticipated transitions beyond the present.

ANALYZING A TRANSITION

Now that you have obtained a panorama of the key transitions in your life, it is time to look intensively at a current or recent transition. You were probably aware as you did the lifeline that transitions have a life of their own. That is, they have a beginning, a middle or turning point, and an ending. For example, Robert was separated from his firm. He had advance warning that a reduction in force would take place and that he would probably be among them (beginning phase). He began to speculate what would happen if and when he would be fired (between phase). When he got the termination notice he was not surprised, but he was angry and confused (present phase). He worried about his future employability and how he would survive financially during the next few months (future phase). He surveyed new career possibilities. He developed a job search plan for his new career choice (finish phase), and soon he found a suitable position. Thus, each life transition has an identifiable beginning, a period of confusion, a clarification, a search, and an exit when the major disruptions of the change are past.

The foregoing model assumes that the transition is experienced in the present time. The phases could also be used in thinking about a past or future transition. In fantasy you could plot the scenario for your transition around these five phases. To make this point more clear, the following activity will help you to review one of your transitions in detail and to extract personal knowledge from it. Using the outline from Table 1-1, choose and analyze a transition you are experiencing presently. Use the example you recalled at the beginning of this chapter. If you do not have a transition clearly at hand, select one from the immediate past or one that you anticipate having in the near future. The purposes of this important activity are to

- understand transitions in general more clearly,
- perceive your personal transition more meaningfully,
- extract learnings from your experience with coping, and
- approach future transitions more confidently and effectively.

In addition to accruing insights from answering the questions in Table 1-1, it would also be helpful to consider the following general questions in the analysis of your transition:

1 Did you *describe* the *problematic situations* of your transition accurately? Analysis of a transition should provide an indication of your personal style of coping with problems. It should also provide a clear awareness of thoughts, feelings, and behavior when confronting problems. For example, do

Table 1-1   Analyzing a Life Transition

Instructions: Preferably, choose a transition you are experiencing currently, or choose one recently experienced. As a third choice, select a transition of someone else or one of your imagination. Then follow the instructions in the six steps.

Step 1: Description
Describe the transition briefly (e.g., your age, the setting, and the nature of the change).

Step 2: The Beginning
Imagine yourself being at the time and in the place where you were first aware of the change or sensed the discontinuity. What were your feelings then?

What were your actions during this time?

How did you cope with this new change initially (e.g., effective problem-solving behaviors that emerged and thoughts and feelings that were managed effectively)?

Step 3: The In-Between Time
Picture the time from the beginning of the transition until now. List some high and low experiences since the beginning of the transition.

Describe what you learned about yourself, about others, or about transitions during this early stage of the transition.

Step 4: The Present
Describe your current feelings about the transition.

What coping attitudes and skills are you using?

What have you learned about yourself, others, or about coping?

Step 5: The Future
As you project your thoughts into the weeks ahead, what do you think will be the high and low points, and how do you expect the transition to be resolved?

How do these thoughtful predictions correspond to your hopes?

What do your hopes reveal about what is important or of value to you?

Step 6: The Finish
What have you learned about yourself, others, and transitions from this whole experience?

How might you gain some personal value (or not gain, or lose) from your transition experiences?

you inhibit the tendency to *act impulsively* when trying to solve the problem; *do nothing*, hoping that it might go away; or do you *gather information* as part of an intentional effort to solve the problem?

2 Do you *recognize* the *values* and *limitations of feelings* as aids to evaluating your transition? A clear awareness of feelings should emerge. For example, when confronting problems do you break into tears or do you become coldly analytical, exhibiting no feelings? Feelings of fear and anger sometimes are cues that a transition is under way or is unduly prolonged. Similarly, do you recognize any sad feelings and realize that you may be grieving? If so, this is a normal and appropriate response to a transition. Individuals vary widely in their emotional responses to transitions, however. The task is to move beyond awareness of feelings to constructive action, using your feelings as a guide. For example, after you accept your feelings of sadness as a normal response to a loss of relationship or job, do you take active thinking steps to let go of the person or job setting emotionally, and do you make plans for a new relationship or work setting?

3 Was your *transition sudden or gradual*? Obviously, if your transition were a surprise, such as sudden job layoff, you would expect more intensity of feeling, perhaps shock and dismay, whereas, in a marital separation, the break may have been coming for a long time. In the latter example, feelings of relief rather than sadness could predominate initially.

4 Did your transition require a *change of role or status*? Painful losses often accompany otherwise pleasurable events, such as retirement. The sudden change from being a powerful person in an organization to one of no status is wrenching for some people. How did you react to the changes of role or status implied in your transition?

5 Was your transition *"on-time" or "off-time"*? Was it planned or was it a movement that did not happen at the expected stage in life? For example, retirement in the mid- or late 60s would be considered on-time, whereas forced early retirement at 45 for disability or job elimination would be considered off-time. The most poignant example of an off-time event would be the death of a young person, whereas death at 80 would be considered more on-time. Emotional reactions to off-time transitions usually would be much more intense than reactions to on-time events.

6 How *long* did your transition *last*? Whether your coping was easy or difficult may have been related to the length of time you had to recover. Unemployment that lasts a year might be considered a painfully long time, whereas an illness that is expected to last a few weeks might be tolerated when one knows that recovery is predictable and imminent. Not knowing the prognosis of a cancer illness, for example, would be a very stressful transition.

7 How many *simultaneous* transitions did you experience? You may have effective coping skills to manage a retirement transition, for example, but if you also move to a new community and have a disabling condition, you might stretch your coping capacity beyond its limit. *A general rule is to limit your transitions to one at a time, if possible.* If the number of transitions happening at one time is beyond your control, it might be helpful to assess your vulner-

ability to such stressors and shore up your coping skills as an alternate strategy.

8 What did you *learn* from previous transitions? Earlier experiences with transitions help. You probably have learned from your previous transitions and could recall the coping strategies that might be applied now. This is true especially if your previous stress management experiences were successful. If your earlier experiences, however, were so severely taxing that they left you with permanent psychological scars, then additional transitional demands might be overwhelming. This situation would call for a competent counselor who specializes in helping people to cope with difficult transitions. Sometimes, too, just the accumulation of little changes leads to an awareness of being overwhelmed. Holmes and Rahe's research on the negative health effects of cumulative life changes is an example.[8] They found that even positive events, such as marriages, vacations, and holidays—along with hassles and arguments—led to vulnerability to health problems.

9 The main question is, how can you gain sufficient *control of your life* so you can *select the timing* of your transitions? How can you plan transitional events such as career change, having children, and moving your residence so that stress effects may be minimized? In addition, the timing of these chosen transitions could be controlled so that time is allowed for those unanticipated life transitions that are likely to be outside your control. For example, Georgia postponed her career change until her youngest child entered school and her husband adjusted to his recent promotion.

10 Where do you *place responsibility* for your transition? Was your transition an event you initiated or encouraged? Was your transition attributable to another person's actions? Did they terminate your employment without cause, for example, or did you see that event coming as an accumulation of irritants and deficiencies? Was society at fault, in your opinion, or do you think that your parents were to blame for your present transition? How you attribute causation for events has implications for how you plan to manage your transition. An important goal during the analysis of a transition is to distinguish between those transitions that were attributable to your responsible choices and those that could be attributed realistically to other persons or events outside your control.

VIEWS OF TRANSITIONAL CHANGE

One of the goals of analyzing your transition is to understand more about the nature of transitions in general. These ways of thinking give you mental structures to explain what is happening as you experience change. Two views are presented here for thinking about your transition.

An Interactional View

Schlossberg described a transition as an interactive process among the person's characteristics and his or her coping resources, the environment, and the nature of the transition itself.[9] We need to look at all of these variables to understand what is going on in a transition. Schlossberg explained coping effectiveness as balancing coping assets and liabilities. For example, two men suddenly are unemployed. One has been offered outplacement counseling, and he systematically undertakes an assessment, planning, and a job search program. The other is offered outplacement counseling also, but he delays and feels depressed much of the time. The problem-solving and planning skills of the second man are low, and his chronic health problems also interfere. The first man has many coping assets and few limiting liabilities, whereas the latter man lacks functional coping skills and has other liabilities for becoming reemployed.

A Process–Stage View

Another view of transition is that it is a process consisting of fairly predictable stages that flow into one another. They often overlap and recycle through earlier stages. This stage model is derived from the literature on dying and was popularized by Kübler-Ross[10] and Parkes.[11] Hopson has taken this basic grieving-process model and adapted it to life transitions in general.[12] The process model used in this book is adapted from Hopson. My discussion of its conceptual development in this chapter and my analysis of the critical points of transition in chapter 2 are based on the work of Kübler-Ross, Parkes, and Hopson.

In general, a transition provokes a response of shock, especially if unplanned. The feelings are usually profound fear and anger. Thoughts usually are disbelief and dismay. Behavior is panic or immobility. This happens, as you may recall, from your experience with a fairly minor loss such as losing your car keys. The crisis of a severe loss is managed by putting our whole being into "neutral" to help assuage the grief. For transitions of lesser import, such as losing the car keys, this first stage is experienced as disorganization of thinking and behavior. Confusion, lack of attention, and feelings of apprehension or annoyance are felt, but it is not usually experienced as a crisis.

Following the short period of mild to severe shock, we typically experience a brief time of profound sadness, and in severe loss, strong feelings of dread. These feelings sometimes alternate with positive feelings, even relief. For example, after a divorce the expected feelings of sadness and loneliness are experienced, but often feelings of pleasure over one's newly found freedom from conflict are also experienced. Often these contradictory feelings oscillate.

These feelings of sadness are usually short-lived, however, and are followed frequently by a period of stabilization of mood and behavior. Our natural healing powers and defenses begin to work at this stage. We minimize any feelings by denying that they are important, or we make excuses to rationalize conflicting feelings. We put up what in some subcultures is called the "stiff upper lip," a determination to "tough it out." There is also a momentary feeling that things are getting better.

Then the reverse usually is experienced. Fears of the future, even catastrophic concerns that this experience will never end, are common. Our self-esteem and our confidence begin to falter. We find ourselves slipping deeper into sadness and pessimism about the future. People experience this period of varying lengths as one of deep sadness and inaction. In counseling terms, we sometimes label it "reactive depression." It is a time when we do not feel like doing anything; energy is low, sleep and appetite are off, and a pervasive feeling of deep sadness is experienced. Reassurances from other people seldom help. We usually want to be alone. From one perspective, this is a natural healing process when reflection and reevaluation take place. It is a time when we can let go of the past—old relationships, values, habits, and things. It is a time of self-discovery of strengths and coping skills.

This process of letting go of the past and taking hold of the new is the key to recovery from a transition. The next stage is to begin this process of taking hold of new relationships and values. It is a time for setting new goals and making fresh plans. Usually this movement from the depressive phase to more positive feelings and optimistic attitudes comes naturally as part of the healing process, and sometimes the depressive phase continues a long time. Occasionally this normal, reactive depression slips into a chronic condition that becomes perpetuated long past the expected healing period. This condition calls for the attention of specialists in managing clinical depression because it requires special psychotherapeutic and sometimes biochemical treatments.

When the tasks of taking hold of new thoughts, feelings, and relationships are undertaken, this process seems to be self-perpetuating. That is, people will begin talking about new goals and aspirations and will make new plans for the future. They will decide to go out among people again, to return to school, learn a new skill, take a trip, or whatever keeps this energy level growing. This growth process typically continues until some other transition or disruptive life experience intervenes. It is hoped that you can, when your transition is well into this stage, look back and ask, "What have I learned about myself and life transitions in this process?" The experience of analyzing your transition earlier in this chapter is aimed in part at understanding this process.

Reporting unpleasant experiences with change is a common theme in literature and is a frequent experience with disillusioned professional sportspeople, business managers, and service professionals.[13] A three-stage process can be used to describe the experiences of these people. The "heroes" go through a process of *departing* (a crisis, trauma, boredom, or anxiety), *initiating* (a search, journey, climb, or career change), and then *returning* (to a new life style, relationship, or career).

This description of the transition process in terms of stages in mourning a loss is very brief. I wish to emphasize again that what I call stages are not fixed and progressive steps. The stages blend into one another, overlap, and repeat in one continuous process. There are also many individual reactions. In chapter 2

I illustrate the process–stage model more fully, take you through a detailed analysis of this process, and make suggestions for managing the special problems that occur at each critical point.

NOTES

1 Ward, B. (1987, July). Managing change. *Sky*, pp. 3–4.
2 Hopson, B., and Adams, J. (1977). Transitions: Defining some boundaries. In J. Adams, J. Hayes, and B. Hopson (Eds.), *Transition*. Montclair, NJ: Allenheld and Osman.
3 Kobassa, S. (1979). Stressful life events, personality and health: An inquiry into hardiness. *Journal of Personality and Social Psychology, 37*, 1–11.
4 Lazarus, R., and Folkman, S. (1984). *Stress, appraisal and coping*. New York: Springer.
5 Jung, C. (1933). *Modern man in search of a soul*. New York: Harcourt, Brace.
6 Bridges, W. (1980). *Transitions: Making sense out of life changes*. Reading, MA: Addison-Wesley.
7 Campbell, J. (1972). *Myths to live by*. New York: Bantam.
8 Holmes, T., and Rahe, R. (1967). The social readjustment rating scale. *Journal of Psychosomatic Research, 11*, 213–218.
9 Schlossberg, N. (1981). A model for analyzing human adaptation to transition. *The Counseling Psychologist, 9*, 2–18.
10 Kübler-Ross, E. (1969). *On death and dying*. New York: Macmillan.
11 Parkes, C. (1972). *Bereavement: Studies of grief in adult life*. New York: International Universities Press.
12 Hopson, B. (1981). Response to papers by Schlossberg, Brammer, and Abrego. *The Counseling Psychologist, 9*, 36–40.
13 Brout, J. (1985, July). Time out. *New Age Journal*, pp. 31–35.

Chapter Two

Managing Your Life Transitions

In this chapter I expand on the process model of phases of reaction to a transition introduced in chapter 1 to describe the critical points of transition. I then present appropriate strategies for coping with these critical points. After studying this chapter you will be able to describe these critical points and to design a self-help program for yourself or a counseling plan for the person you are helping. Thus, the process model provides a map through the transition.

LENGTH AND SEVERITY OF RESPONSES TO A TRANSITION

The length and severity of responses to a transition are dependent on many factors. Research specialists have called these determining factors mediating variables. These variables are

- the *meaning* of the transition for you,
- the extent to which you *express your feelings* about the transition,
- the use of *previous experiences* with transitions, and

• the extent and functioning of your *support system* and other *coping resources*.

As I describe the six critical points of transition in the following sections, I will explain how these mediating variables affect your transition.

You probably are aware from reading the reflections on life transitions that were presented in chapter 1 that you face three general choices. Suppose that there are multiple and distressing changes in your work setting. You can choose to do one of the following:

• Change the *situation* (e.g., change jobs).
• Change the *meaning* of the situation (e.g., see change in your work as a challenge rather than a threat).
• Change *reactions* to the situation (e.g., adjust or cope rather than be frustrated or angry).

There are a number of general responses you could make to a transition that would help you to manage the critical points. The key to making one of the three choices just suggested is your perception of the power you have over yourself and your environment. You can choose to empower yourself by perceiving yourself as a person of importance, competence, and influence.

Research has revealed additional personal reactions that affect the outcome of a transition. In a study of "hardy copers," Kobassa identified three kinds of copers. *Committed* people knew their values and goals and pursued them diligently. *Controlled* people perceived that they were in control of their lives and sought to empower themselves with this sense of control. *Challenged* people perceived disruptive changes as challenges to growth.[1] Frankl's studies of the responses of people in Nazi concentration camps revealed that not only did the horrible conditions provoke the suffering, but also the way in which these conditions were perceived.[2] Survivors were able to tell themselves that, although they could not control the conditions, they could control their reactions to those conditions.

Possession of the coping skills listed in chapter 1 also determines how effectively you can manage the critical stages of your transitions. So, how you react personally to transitions is a complex mixture of mediating variables in the transition event and your personal style. These points in the process are labeled "critical" because what is not done or what is done as self-help or counseling determines whether or not the transition will work out satisfactorily.

A PROCESS-STAGE MODEL OF TRANSITION

Figure 2-1 depicts the process-stage model of transition that I have been discussing. The vertical axis represents the level of a person's mood and self-esteem as he or she moves through each stage of transition, the center point

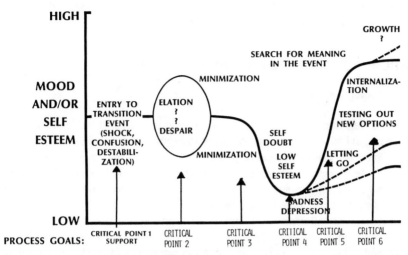

Figure 2-1 A process–stage model of transition. (From Hopson, B. (1981). Response to papers by Schlossberg and Brammer. *The Counseling Psychologist, 9,* 3. Adapted by permission of publisher and author.)

being the balance between sad and happy moods. The horizontal axis represents the process of movement through time and through the mourning process inherent in the transition experience, identified as six critical points. The U-shaped curve depicted in this model illustrates how the process of adjustment to a transition moves from high personal integration, to disorganization and distress (a downward movement of mood and self-esteem), back up to integration. The dotted lines indicate that a stage may continue for a long time.

This model is useful in that it helps people to organize transition experiences in a way that conforms to their life experiences. For the professional counselor, it offers an explanatory road map to help people put their feelings and experiences into words and to make sense out of their transitions. The model makes familiar what is often mysterious and frightening. Because the transition experience appears to be such strange and threatening territory, we often think our experiences are unique. Yet, it is important to realize that we share much in common with other people.

This model should be used with caution. Research specialists Silver and Wortman offered special warnings not to overgeneralize from the curve depicted in Figure 2-1.[3] This transition curve is based on evidence from examples in counseling practice. It is a generalized curve that applies very widely to all transitional changes. There are many individual variations, however. Some stages are skipped, for example; others are repeated in circular fashion. Some people remain fixed at a particular stage.

The remainder of this chapter is divided into six parts, each dealing with one of the six critical points of transition depicted in Figure 2-1. In addition to describing the typical responses that people have to the stages, I describe strategies for self-help and for helping professionals.

CRITICAL POINT 1: ENTERING THE TRANSITION

Typical Responses

The initial reaction to a transition depends on the severity and suddenness of the experience at entry. The first critical point in Figure 2-1 represents an event that is perceived as a crisis. Typical responses to sudden and severe entry are shock, speechlessness, panic, and dread. These reactions are followed by sensations of numbness or feeling drained, isolated, and abandoned. Occasionally, no feeling is experienced in this state of numbness.

If a less critical transition is involved, people typically experience confusion, anxiety, momentary inefficiency (such as forgetting), and a sense of being constricted. This awareness of constriction is sometimes expressed in an image such as being "boxed in" or "squeezed" between two large rocks. Our language defies precise description of these poignant human experiences, so we use images.

Our cultural background also determines how we respond to this critical point. Some people, for example, are rather stoic and accept crises and suffering as commonplace life experiences. Others perceive almost every change as a crisis. Occasionally, a reflective person sees the entry into a transition as a predictable ending to a previous life style, relationship, or important value. For example, I have heard people whose employment has been terminated say, "I saw it coming; I knew I would need to make some changes; this event decided it for me."

Self-Help Strategies and Strategies for Helping Professionals

If entering a transition involves crisis, then crisis management strategies need to be applied immediately. An event is labeled a crisis when it unexpectedly and severely disrupts our life routines. Usually we feel frustrated, and perhaps also distressed and helpless. Crises usually are of short duration, however, because people's automatic protective mechanisms emerge when they are under acute strain. Crises are characterized by four features.

They

- provoke anxiety rapidly,
- mobilize our coping resources,
- lead to disruption of our thoughts and acts, and
- reach resolution fairly quickly.

My recommended general helping strategies for dealing with crises are as follows:

- Assess the nature and severity of the event accurately.
- Inventory your resources, or the other person's resources for coping.
- Decide on the best form of help needed now.
- Act in a directly helpful way (using methods suggested in this section).
- Work toward stabilization and resolution of the emotional impact.

Assess the Crisis It is helpful to identify the kind of crisis you are experiencing. Is it *developmental*, such as the birth of a child or leaving home for college? These are normal crises, expected as a part of living. *Transitional* crises may set off emotions connected with earlier developmental problems. For example, one of the partners of a marriage had a severe early family problem that caused the partners to mistrust each other. Prior to their separation the partners were suspicious of one another, but this mild mistrust did not interfere with their lives. Now that a divorce is formally taking place, the old feelings of suspicion and gross mistrust are triggered and add to the mistrust fomented by the present transition. The significance of this example is to alert us to the possibility that earlier developmental crises can complicate the current transitional crisis. Most of us think of crises as *situational*—those conditions of severe and sometimes sudden losses such as being fired from a job, becoming ill, or suffering an accident. This situational type is the focus of helping strategies described here.

Existential crises refer to anxious feelings experienced when facing important decisions or committing ourselves to responsible actions. These decisions bring up old unresolved conflicts and feelings about the purpose of life, importance of possessions, and freedom of choice, for example. An existential crisis is a normal accompaniment to living. Existential choices become crises when we are aware of the difference between where we are now and new possibilities for our lives. Transitions often provoke existential crises that earlier had been avoided or tentatively resolved.

It is prudent to plan for coping with these tag ends of unresolved existential questions when the crisis of the moment eases. If this resolution is not done, these conflicts tend to reappear at most unwelcome times, or they will be experienced as anxiousness, boredom, or purposelessness. John, for example, was very distressed about losing his job at age 42. He appeared to be bored and anxious for about three months following termination. Discussion revealed that he was struggling with old feelings—questions about his personal worth, purpose of his life, and future goals.

The good news about crises is that they shake us up so that we are forced to look at our lives differently. Furthermore, crises usually are short-lived. When in the throes of a crisis, however, it is difficult to see options and growth possibilities. We must wait patiently for the perspective that comes at a later stage so that we can see the meaning in the critical event. It is usually reassuring to note that your coping skills and psychological defenses come to your rescue during a crisis. If your reserves are not adequate to the crisis, however, and you experience dysfunctional behaviors such as attention and memory problems, do not hesitate to seek psychological help. Most professional helpers follow a "multiple impact strategy." This means doing several things at once: giving support to the person, working with the family, and utilizing other helping specialists.

Giving and Receiving Support   As supportive relatives or friends or as helping professionals, we must trust our intuitive judgment about what is needed. The key to appropriate support is sensing what people need from observing their actions. Sometimes sitting silently with a person is all that is needed at that moment—what I call "presencing". Sometimes a light touch, like a gentle hand on the arm or an arm around the shoulder, is helpful. Again, these specific suggestions are determined as much by the social customs of your culture as they are by your perceptions of the person's present needs. Touching, for example, is taboo in some settings and very much appreciated in others. If you are a professional helper, your state laws may prohibit touching. These strict laws grew out of abuses by unscrupulous helping professionals.

Relatives or friends who have basic helping skills are essential. How one gives or receives support is an individual matter, so it is difficult to prescribe rules. In chapter 3 I describe more fully how support can be given and how networks can be built to provide support in transitions. If you are going through this early critical phase of a transition, seek those persons on whom you can depend to give what you want. If you are helping others in this phase, imagine what it would be like for you and then respond empathically. Appropriately helpful responses emerge when we trust the wisdom of our total being to guide us. Sometimes, however, you will need to ask people what they need. What is often overlooked is that people usually want space and time to react to the transition and to grieve alone. So, it is prudent to determine what the person needs and wants now. If we cannot infer what they need, then ask them.

Releasing Emotions   One of the helpful things you can do for yourself during the early grieving time of a crisis is to give yourself permission to fall apart. This means expressing any feelings that you are experiencing. It means acting strangely and thinking crazy thoughts, if you are so inclined. Conversely, if you are helping others through this crises point, it is reassuring to give them permission to fall apart. There are strong norms in some groups that favor control and putting up a brave front. Although this may stabilize the situation momentarily, there usually is a heavy price to pay later for this kind of denial and control. This price is likely to be unexplained periods of weeping, anger, and panic later in the process. It is important to realize that at this point of grieving, people often experience emotional upset, disordered thinking, and disrupted sleeping and eating habits.

Listening to and Expressing Feelings   Listen for apt descriptive language in yourself or others, especially the use of metaphors. These are very expressive images that tell much about how you or others are experiencing the transition at this moment. For example, one person said, "The bottom has just dropped out of my life." Others have said, "I feel like I'm squeezed in a big vise," or "I'm detached from my moorings—I feel I'm drifting helplessly." It is usually more comfortable to express feeling in these images than to say directly, "I'm scared," or "I'm angry."

Images also provide useful entry points to the person's present inner world. Telling you how things seem to them in images or stories is an invitation to further exploration. You will find it productive to inquire about what their "vise" or "squeezing" is like, for example. Sometimes it is helpful to suggest an image to the person that you think captures the essence of their experiences, such as "it seems like you have just been pushed over a cliff; is that right?"

Conversely, we should not assume that everyone entering a sudden transition is thrust into a crisis. It is tempting to project our own experiences with loss to the other person. For example, in trying to empathize we might go too far and see their loss exactly as we experienced our transitions. Awareness of this possibility is the best prevention of unwarranted projection. In any case, too much energy usually is invested in the triggering event, and special efforts are needed to move on.

For some people entering a transition, there may be momentary relief from a previously demanding situation or unsatisfying relationship. The death of a parent suffering from a long illness may be experienced with a sense of relief, for example. Feelings of loneliness, sadness, anger, and anxiety may come later in the process. The important principle here for managing your own transitions is to be in close touch with your feelings and to seek someone in your support network with whom to discuss them. If you are the helper, then it is important to encourage others to express their feelings, if they want to do so. We must be able to sense when they are ready to talk, and then give them encouragement. If we incorrectly judged their readiness, they will usually tell us. It is important to realize that even in fairly trivial life changes, there is a measure of transition shock and modified grieving. We must be open to a wide variety of emotional reactions at this entry point.

CRITICAL POINT 2:
EXPERIENCING CYCLICAL FEELINGS

Typical Responses

Critical Point 2 usually comes shortly after the initial reactions to the transition. Depending on the severity of the triggering event, the first stage is brief, followed by expressed feelings of dread, anger, sadness, or fear. These feelings may alternate with relief, sometimes euphoria. The cyclical nature of these feelings is depicted as an oval on the process–stage model (see Figure 2-1). The reason this point is labeled "critical" is that it is a very confusing experience for grieving people. They are baffled by the contradictory nature of their experiences of sadness and relief. Some people experience this period as an oscillation between sadness and relief. For example, Alex and Alicia were undergoing a divorce. After a separation involving a long period of conflict, their reaction was a mixture of alternating pleasurable relief with the sadness of separation. Similarly, after caring for a loved one during a long period of suffering there is a feeling of relief along with the sadness of their death. This feeling is confusing and fearsome; yet it is reassuring to know that this experience is common.

This second stage is considered critical also because many fears are experienced as one contemplates the future. The grieving person experiences waves of pessimism, and sometimes fear of the future takes on catastrophic qualities. For example, expressions like "this is the end for me; I'll never get over this loss; thoughts of the future panic me" are usual.

Sometimes the emotional experience at the end of Stage 2 is one of calm confidence that the worst is over. The body has been in neutral during the shock stage, and now functions are getting back to normal. Psychological defenses such as denial, fantasy, and rationalization have emerged to cope with the panic and dread. Strengths, such as courage and hope, are mobilized also. Then it hits just when you think you are on top! Often without warning, feelings of despair, lowered self-esteem, and uncontrollable anger appear again. This event ushers in Critical Point 3—further minimization of feelings and slipping self-esteem.

Self-Help Strategies and Strategies
for Helping Professionals

Expressing Feelings The most effective means toward self-help—and helping others—for Critical Stage 2 is to encourage expression of emotions and to describe body experiences, such as pains and pressures. While the person you are helping expresses feelings of confusion, sadness, or relief, it is important to listen attentively and reflect the basic message about what the person is experiencing. For example, we might say, "Although you feel very sad about this separation, I sense your feelings of relief, too." As a result, awareness of how one feels is increased; people feel understood and accepted, their feelings are validated, and they are assured that it is permissible to feel this way.

Expressing feelings is especially difficult when coping with a severe loss, such as a death. There are so many demands on survivors, especially if they are surviving parents. There is little time to fall apart because children must be cared for, arrangements must be made for funerals, and one must get back into productive work and on with the business of living. Although these tasks help in the healing process, they often sidetrack essential expression of feelings. Jane, for example, whose husband died, was faced with so many demands that she could not grieve her loss. As a single parent she had many immediate tasks of support and maintenance. She just could not afford to fall apart emotionally. Placing this lid on her feelings was her historical life style for coping with losses, so it was easier during this crisis to hold her feelings in. At some point, however, she needed a supportive friend or professional counselor who could help her express the feelings that were held in by such tight control.

Reassurance Another helpful goal at this point is for you to feel, or to communicate to the other person, that these feelings are normal. They are common human experiences in the course of grieving over a loss. It is normal, for example, to feel sad but relieved, guilty, afraid, or angry at the same time. Conventional advice often indicates that one should "control" feelings, "be strong," and "keep a stiff upper lip." Western social customs allow free expression of sad feelings, but expressing anger—especially toward the separated person—is taboo. It is important to realize that it is becoming socially acceptable and necessary for mental health to express any feeling one is experiencing.

Interpretation Explaining the normal course of grieving is often helpful. At Critical Point 2 grieving people are usually over the most intense emotional reactions to the change and are open to discussing what they are experiencing. Descriptions of how the normal course of grieving takes place, including cautions about individual variations, allow the healing process to begin. This kind of discussion reassures the person that this healing process is predictable and that it usually has positive outcomes. Frank discussion encourages the person to live through the process hopefully and courageously instead of pessimistically and evasively.

It is the unknown that distresses us, and it is very reassuring to realize that these events are reasonably predictable. Certainly, awareness of how the process of coping with loss evolves provides a buffer against the five "dangerous Ds" characteristic of the later Critical Stage 4:

- depression (more severe mood than normal sadness),
- discomfort (agitation and distressing bodily reactions),
- dread (intense fear of the future),
- despair (sense of hopelessness), and
- depersonalization (loss of clear image of self).

Discussions about the nature of change and healing processes also help the person to manage "survivor guilt." This is an emotional reaction of people who experience a severe loss, such as in an accident in which they are the survivors. They wonder, "Why was I spared?" Similarly, an understanding of the mourning process helps to deal with "victim bitterness." This common reaction after loss leaves the person angry over the event and resultant pain. It is another version of the "Why me?" response. Understanding how change affects us and how the healing process is facilitated help greatly to ease these feelings of guilt and anger.

CRITICAL POINT 3: MINIMIZING FEELINGS

Typical Responses

Denial   At Critical Point 3 our natural psychological defenses are well mobilized. This defense posture takes the form of minimizing the experience of loss. For example, we might deny the feeling of pain and say something like, "I'm OK; don't worry about me, I'll get along." We realize that we have a problem posed by the change, but we are not ready or willing to face it just yet. We may also have daydreams about a better life.

Although extreme and persistent denial of feelings would have unhealthy consequences, denial serves a useful purpose momentarily. It enables us to mobilize our strengths and to manage the pain of change and loss. Denial forms the basis of hope and reduces fear. Toughing it out has survival value because denial is a buffer against the ravages of further change.

Denial can be persistent and counterproductive, however. It can move readily into escape devices, such as persistent fantasies about better times or relationships. The idea that change can be reversed, or that conditions as they were before the change can be restored are additional consequences of denial. We sometimes believe, for example, that the lost relationship can be reestablished, or that the lost job can be regained.

Disbelief   Disbelief is another potential problem for us at Critical Point 3. If prolonged, the refusal to accept the reality of the loss can cause later problems in the healing process. "Why" questions pervade our thinking, such as "Why did this happen to me?" Guilt persists in the form of regret: "If I'd only (taken better care, sought a physician, talked to the employer, and so forth)." Religious values might be useful to consider here. Kushner's book, *When Bad Things Happen to Good People*, is an attempt to help people reconcile destructive changes with virtuous images of themselves.[4] For example, a person with a diagnosis of leukemia says, "Why? I've done everything right all my life—no smoking, plenty of exercise, good diet, and generally right living."

For some people, the phrase "It is the will of God" aids their coping and comfort. Whereas it is comforting for some, this belief is distressing or appears evasive for others. For example, a person loses a loved one in an accident. They say to themselves, "I must accept this event since it is the will of God. I should not feel upset." A likely negative consequence is that people who say this deny themselves the healing process of mourning their loss. They subordinate their feelings to thought manipulation designed to explain their losses. In addition, if the mourning process is short circuited by such thought manipulations, people deny their need for support from friends or professionals. They keep their feelings inside, which is likely to retard their healing. Ideally, the healing process is facilitated by a combination of comforting thoughts that help make sense out of an otherwise meaningless event, and comforting support from talking with family and friends. It is important to believe that reaching out to others is not a sign of weakness, but a useful strength. In any case, it is my firm opinion that in trying to be helpful we should never say to a person experiencing loss that "It is the will of God."

Hope Hope is the antidote to despair and helps make crises more tolerable. Hope is based on a firm belief or assumption that things will get better. We could dismiss hopeful thoughts as wishful thinking, or we could view hope as a positive expectancy that conditions will probably improve. Medical folklore contains many examples of how such positive expectancies aided unexplainable recovery from physical illness. Hope involves strong imagery of the desired outcome. We must have such outcomes clearly outlined in mental pictures to sustain our hope. The limitation of such a view of hope is that it could easily slip into fantasy wishes about the future, thus serving as an escape from present realities and responsibilities. It could also mislead the person with strong denial of reality in a terminal illness, for example. Giving up wishes may be disappointing, but giving up hope makes us vulnerable to doubt, despair, helplessness, and, finally, dysfunction.

Anger Feelings are still strong during this stage in the healing process. Anger is often experienced but is seldom expressed. We resent a person leaving us, for example. We get angry with the employer for firing us. We resent things happening without our permission—"How come?" Often we are just angry, not knowing precisely what we are angry about or toward whom. Perhaps you have felt, at times, like lashing out at the world indiscriminately. This is normal anger seeking expression.

Fear Sometimes, catastrophic fears of the future persist when the reality of the loss seeps into our awareness. Pessimistic messages keep repeating, like "Things can't get better, they can only get worse." "I'll never get over this experience." This is normal fear seeking expression and emerging as pessimism about the future.

Control Occasionally, our feelings are so well defended that we think all conditions are under control and that our situation can only improve. It would be inhuman to minimize or discourage this calmness and confidence; we should, however, be alert in ourselves and others to the strong possibility that this stabilization is illusory and temporary, and that "it" will hit us—*it* being the return sweep of feelings described earlier. One consequence is that our future probably would look bleak again, and at worst we would start blaming ourselves for the negative feelings.

Self-Help Strategies and Strategies for Helping Professionals

Maintaining Self-esteem Your basic goal at this stage is to maintain self-esteem. This is done through affirmations—self-messages saying that you are a person of worth and dignity. You tell yourself over and over that you can choose to feel confident of yourself, or you can choose to give up and become depressed. This is not to deny feelings of sadness and anxiety, however. These feelings can be experienced without decline of self-worth or fears of sinking into the black hole of despondency and dread of the future. One way to affirm one's self is to prepare cards with messages such as "I am confident," "I am a successful person," "I am loving and caring." Then place them in prominent locations at home, or take time to read and repeat them at regular intervals.

Expressing Feelings Another helping strategy is to encourage expression of feelings experienced now—the fear, anger, guilt, frustration, and confusion. This expression not only helps to reduce the intensity and debilitating effects of the emotions but also opens doors to hope and optimism.

Maintaining Health An important consideration at all stages, but particularly at Point 3 because of acute stress, is health maintenance. The usual rules prevail—adequate rest, good diet, tension reduction, and vigorous exercise consonant with physical limitations. When self-esteem begins to slip, and depressive feelings creep in, motivation for health maintenance often declines. Therefore, a most helpful strategy at this point is to force yourself to maintain your optimum health.

Stabilizing Existence Keeping your life as stabilized as possible at this point is the best advice we can give ourselves and others. There is a temptation to initiate many changes—changing residence, taking a trip, or returning to school, for example. Conventional wisdom says, "Keep busy, keep moving." Yet, adding more stressful changes to your life at this stage adds to the transition shock. I repeat a general rule cited earlier for managing transitions successfully: one change at a time. A corollary of this rule is that if additional changes take place beyond our control, that we accept them.

Keeping busy in meaningful activity may be helpful, however, as a first aid gesture. It keeps your attention focused outside yourself, not on the dark recesses of your personality. Keep in mind, however, that keeping busy is a temporary and evasive expedient at best until you can get on with the main business of healing and helping.

Assessing Coping Skills During this critical time there are moments when you are calm, lucid, rational, and hopeful. This is a good time to assess your coping skills described in chapter 1. Identifying the dependable people in your social network is especially important during severe loss and profound change. These significant others hold an important key to unlocking the healing process to come, just as they were during the two earlier critical points.

Restructuring our negative thought patterns such as "I can't cope," "I'm weak," or "I'm no good" is another essential skill. Are you giving yourself structured, supportive messages like, "I can cope," "I am a strong person," "I have many strengths," "I am a valuable person," and "I am not a victim"? Similarly, perceiving ourselves as responsible for controlling our thoughts and actions is an important kind of awareness. As was indicated previously, a key healing task is to find an optimal view of control in your life. One extreme view is that you control everything that happens to you—that you are totally responsible for your life. The other extreme is that you are the victim of circumstances or fate, and that you have little control over your life. Successful copers are somewhere in the middle, but basically they declare that they are in control of their lives.

Some people with strong religious convictions that God is controlling their lives would have difficulty with the coping attitude that we control our lives. This view is similar to the "will of God" belief discussed earlier. Some people appear to work out a reasonably satisfactory reconciliation of this conflict of views. They seem to be saying that as a practical matter I must control my life, but there is a plan or will that transcends my own that I trust will be revealed to me in time. In the meantime, I need not sit by helplessly waiting for the will of God to become known. If this is a conflict for you, how do you plan to resolve it? What belief system about control works best for you?

This is an appropriate stage to practice your problem-solving skills and to expand your repertoire of problem-solving methods. In chapter 4 you will be asked to work on these essential coping skills. The flexible problem solver has many alternative strategies from which to choose when the preferred method does not work. Thus, you can avoid the plight of the hapless Indian monkey. Hunters placed rice in a hollow coconut attached to a stake. The hole was just large enough for the monkey to insert its paw. When the monkey grasped a handful of rice it could not withdraw its paw without releasing the rice. Reluctant to do so, the monkey held on to the rice rigidly until the hunter returned with his sack. Do you know of problematic situations in which you acted like the monkey? It is important here to understand our stressful, angry outbursts and your baffling touchiness at this time. Unless these coping strategies for managing your feelings at Critical Point 3 are understood and applied, conflict with significant others in your life is inevitable.

CRITICAL POINT 4:
MANAGING DEPRESSION AND SEARCHING
FOR MEANING

Typical Responses

As self-esteem decreases, accompanying feelings of depression tend to increase. As I indicated earlier, it is not essential to the healing process to go into a deep and prolonged depression. It appears that how we handle our normal sadness about our loss is the critical consideration at this point. Even though you do not experience a severe depression (and depressions are labeled clinically as mild, moderate or severe), the world certainly looks grim and grey. Motivation for doing anything declines, sleep and eating disturbances increase, and mood is persistently low no matter who is present or what is done.

Depending on previous life style, alcohol and drug use may increase. Even prescriptive drugs (tranquilizers for jumpiness and antidepressants for mood) are controversial. Whether you should take one or the other depends much on individual needs and the considered judgment of a knowledgeable physician. In the interest of reducing suffering, however, it appears that treatment errors usually are made on the side of too much medication.

Searching for Meaning   A critical question here is how should you interpret the meaning of this stage in the change process? I maintain that going along with the depressed state is a natural way to take time out. The shock of change and wrestling with the feelings experienced earlier take a heavy energy toll. The result is depletion and exhaustion. This lethargic period thus offers time for replenishment and healing. I emphasize the word *time*, because this replenishment cannot be rushed through without risks of relapse into prolonged and severe depression. How one interprets and handles this awkward and painful stage is critical.

Another key question is what is considered a normal or usual length of time for the depressive stage? This is impossible to answer because it is determined by cultural norms, life experiences, temperament, nature of the triggering event, and the state of coping skills. Typically, for severe losses several months are needed to complete the healing process.

This depressive stage is interpreted in many different ways by those experiencing loss. Some view it as fearful and try to avoid it; others seem to do everything to extend their depression. The length and severity of depression is unpredictable because it is so easy to reward depressive behavior, hence to prolong it. For example, talking about how awful I feel or focusing on how miserable I am tends to prolong the sad feelings. It seems contradictory in light of earlier discussions about expressing feelings, to say that talking extensively about how bad one feels keeps the bad feeling going; however, talking about depression usually gets much attention and sympathy, so people are reluctant to give it up.

Regardless of individual differences in interpreting and responding to depressive feelings at this critical point, almost all people report experiences of being "out of it," meaning being detached from events and realities around them. Activities usually considered pleasant lose their enjoyment. Hobbies are no longer attractive or absorbing. Again, one interpretation of this experience is that we need some space—some neutral time to reflect and do other things to heal ourselves. We need time to let go of the past and grasp new possibilities for the future.

This experience of a neutral zone when nothing much seems to be going on in our lives is baffling to us. Our "shoulds" come to awareness; we feel that we should be doing *something*. The idea of just taking time off to do nothing does not make sense to people accustomed to productive work all the time. The African Kikuyus have a phrase that explains why they periodically go off to the bush alone for extended periods. They say it is to "let their souls catch up with their bodies." Similarly, after experiencing a change we need time to think and regroup our energies. We need to reflect on what the transition meant to us, to let the pain or discomfort subside, and to prepare for new experiences. Because the reactions and meanings of this stage are so variable, it is difficult to cite a neat helping strategy for ourselves or those we are helping through this difficult time. Some of the methods that have been helpful are described in the next section.

Self-Help Strategies and Strategies for Helping Professionals

Encouragement Suggesting that we go with the feelings we are experiencing is often helpful. Be sad, for example, rather than deny that such feelings exist. Encouraging people to be aware of how these feelings are experienced in their bodies is helpful. Typically, aches and pains, pressures, and tensions are experienced in unique, individual form, but a general malaise or lack of energy is a common experience.

When experiencing a lack of motivation and energy, it is helpful to realize in ourselves, as well as when helping others, that we should take time out from demanding responsibilities and delay planning for the future. Conventional advice often urges us to get active, take a trip, go to school, or sell the house, for example. These may be useful strategies later, but for now give yourself (and others) permission to do nothing for a while. Focus on self-maintenance and keep everyday tasks simple.

Encouraging self-nourishment is very effective. This means do something you enjoy or did enjoy in the past. Self-nourishment means focusing on sensory pleasures, such as having your hair done, buying flowers, listening to favorite music, getting a massage, eating your favorite foods, or buying new clothes. In fact, one of the most prominent treatments for severe clinical depression is to focus on experiencing pleasurable events. A person in a transition workshop said, with a twinkle in her eyes, that she was under so much strain and felt so down from all the recent changes in her life that she was going out the next weekend to do "something decadent."

Some people believe that suffering is a virtuous quality of living and that character is strengthened through adversity. It is difficult to help such people see that they can modify their belief somewhat so they can allow themselves pleasure also. It may be necessary to explain why it is important to nourish themselves for a while, to shuck outside responsibilities and take time just "to be."

Reflecting and Keeping a Journal   In the early stages of this neutral period it may not be appropriate to talk much about the meaning of the experience, but if you are experiencing this stage it is important to watch for cues when you are ready to do some reflection, keep a journal, or think of the future. Meditation is important not only as a method of managing tensions, but also as openness to insights and messages. Specific suggestions for meditation are described in chapter 5.

Not only does writing your experiences in a journal preserve them for later reflection, but also the act of recording your thoughts and feelings in itself is helpful. This can be a simple diary with a free flow of ideas and feelings, or it can be a more structured experience with descriptions of crossroads faced and paths taken. Progoff has designed such a formal process called "process meditation," which you might find helpful to guide your meditation and writing.[5] Others find writing poetry or stories helpful. Reading comforting and inspirational literature sometimes helps to reduce tension and discover meaning.

Alone and Social Time   Having time alone is important at this point, but there are times when discussions with a friend or professional helper are indicated. Most people prefer a balance of alone time and supportive conversations. Therefore, you need to plan for this alone time, forcing out pressures to keep busy. Even though it seems painful at first to force yourself to be alone, it is essential to the healing process. If you are helping others through this phase, they may need your understanding of their loneliness and your encouragement to face their alone time courageously.

Getting Stuck   What if you or the person you are helping does not have a severe depression but seems to be stuck in the sad feelings? Psychologists have a number of methods to help you move toward goals of growth and emotional stability. Their methods have some implications for self-help. The references offer additional reading if you decide to investigate further. Remember that, like all helpful methods, they are limited when misapplied.

Centering is a method described by Gendlin to focus on the bodily experience of the feeling.[6] You go into the sensation or "felt sense" of the sadness, for example, by describing what it feels like in your body—the lump in your throat or the weight on your shoulders. This experience leads to greater awareness of what is going on, offers some release of tension, and generates increased motivation to keep growing.

Logotherapy was developed by Frankl out of his devastating experiences in a World War II concentration camp.[7] The basic idea, originating in ancient Greek Stoic philosophy, is that suffering is a subjective experience as well as a reaction to an objective event. Thus, it is not always the way things are that leads to suffering; it is sometimes our reactions to those events. Frankl emphasized that although we cannot always change the tragic circumstances of our lives, we can choose how we are going to react to those events. In this sense we have freedom and meaning; this awareness of freedom to choose and override tragedy constitutes what Frankl called the "triumphant power of the human spirit." There are several specialized helping methods, called logotherapy, that flow from Frankl's basic idea about finding meaning in suffering.[8]

Encouraging people to reexperience the feelings about a person or event helps them to get closer to their feelings. In a relaxed state people can be encouraged to focus on tag ends of their feelings. Then they are encouraged to experience them more strongly. When the feelings finally emerge, usually after prolonged denial, they are discussed openly. So, it is basically a method for helping people who have difficulty expressing feelings to experience and express their feelings.

Methods of authoritative exhortation are used in much of the world for people who persist in their depressive states. In a caring but firm manner they are told by a person in authority that they have, indeed, had a sad experience, but that they have been depressed long enough, and now they will be expected back on the job the next morning. Although this method makes the questionable assumption that people have total voluntary control over their depressive feelings, it helps to break the cycle of reward for mild depressions associated with transitions.

In my opinion, exhortation methods are a last resort. It is more useful to help depressed people see that they have more to gain by not being depressed than by staying where they are. A strategy used by behavior-change specialists is to ask, "What do you need to *do* to feel better?" The focus is not on further attention to the depressed behavior, but on what can be done differently that will result in feeling better. More specific methods for helping the depressed to change their self-defeating thoughts and behaviors are described in chapter 4.

Severe and Persistent Depression

From your personal experience and observations you have probably realized that depression can last a long time. Earlier life experiences, a host of personality factors, and health conditions determine the length of a depressive episode. If such is the case for you or the person you are helping, referral to a competent professional helper is indicated. Psychiatrists, because of their legal authority to prescribe medication, are the specialists of choice in severe and prolonged depressions. Some depressed people need a combination of psychological counseling and medication to enable them to function better on the job and in their families, and to generally improve the quality of their lives.

Specialists sometimes have difficulty diagnosing depression accurately and treating it effectively. All of the suggestions in this book pertain to the ordinary sadness that accompanies transitional changes. This type of depression usually lifts in time regardless of what we do or do not do. This natural process is reassuring, but we need to be alert to the possibility that such a depression will continue for a long time, will become more severe, or will return at a later time.

CRITICAL POINT 5: LETTING GO AND TAKING HOLD OF NEW PLANS

Typical Responses

The critical quality of this stage resides in its tentativeness and fragility. Efforts to reach out as described previously are easily defeated. We saw how difficult it is to pull out of a depression and, when this happens, one is torn by the conflict between moving on and holding back.

The second critical quality of this stage for some vulnerable people is self-destruction. I do not wish to unduly alarm you, but research on suicide indicates that this is the time people should be alert to the possibility of suicide attempts.[9] This could take place in the preceding depressive stage also, but it is more likely to appear when life seems to be getting better. There are several possible reasons why this might be so. One is that in the depressive stage people have low energy. It takes considerable energy to make plans for self-destruction, and even more to carry them out. In addition, as described earlier, there are many rewards for being depressed, so some people are reluctant to disturb this condition. We also probably get out of some responsibilities like work and expectations for high performance. If we are depressed we need not take chances on failure by doing anything risky. We tell ourselves, "After all, what can you expect of a person who feels so down?"

Again, I wish to emphasize that you need not fret about your own or another's possibility of suicidal actions. Thoughts about suicide are fairly common at this stage, largely because we realize that we must begin to take responsibility for our behavior. Responsible action is not an attractive option for many people. Fortunately for you and me, there is a strong force in people that appears to propel them into constructive action. Even if people seem to do nothing to bring themselves out of their depressive state, a natural healing process takes place. The key elements of this process of healing are increases in self-esteem, letting go of the past, new ideas for growth, and optimism about the future.

Another thought about the possibility of suicide bears mention before going on. In addition to being alert to this possibility in ourselves and others, it is prudent to have someone in your support network whom you could call to talk about this life or death decision. It is difficult to decide alone because we easily lose our perspective, and we tend to make decisions impulsively. Seeking a psychologist or psychiatrist would be most appropriate for people who persistently threaten suicide or for experiencing these feelings yourself. If you live in a metropolitan area there is likely to be a crisis hotline you could call. Crisis center staff members can be most helpful at times when life looks bleak or hopeless. Their understanding, help in exploring alternatives, and possibly referring you to a specialist are important resources.

On a positive note, you can expect to feel better without outside help or much personal effort. One characteristic of this critical stage is that the letting-go and taking-hold process described in chapter 1 begins to make sense. You will be aware that now you can give yourself permission to release the hold of that past relationship, job, or value. You will find that you can let go without feeling that you are cheating yourself. For example, you will find that you can retain memories of the lost relationship but can give up expectations that it will return. Consequently, you will be released from the energy-consuming emotional conflict.

The realization that others do not own you and that you are your own person is an enormously freeing consequence of this letting-go experience. Their expectations and demands are not binding. You will feel in control of your life again. In addition, you will be able to look ahead and see possibilities for a new life more clearly.

A basic question here is, "How can the twin processes of letting go and taking hold be accelerated without doing violence to the healing process?" In part, the answer lies in trusting our thinking capacities. For example, it is at about this stage in the process when we sense that the change we experienced represents a new beginning. Yet, this beginning imposed by the transition is really an ending: the ending of a previous life style or relationship. This realization that the transition is ending helps us to let go of the past and permits us to seek a new life style or relationship. Thus, the second stage of awareness takes place when we see all changes as endings, and when we perceive that these endings are also beginnings. T.S. Eliot put it succinctly in "Little Gidding": "What we call the beginning is often the end;/And to make an end is to make a beginning;/The end is where we start from."[10] Cultural norms determine the speed of this healing process, because they usually dictate what we do in a transition. I am suggesting that we look beyond these customs and decide for ourselves or those we are helping what is best for us or for them.

Self-Help Strategies and Strategies for Helping Professionals

Reinforcing Efforts When that first inkling of impending change for the better creeps into your awareness, nourish and expand it! Give yourself encouraging messages such as "I'm more hopeful now," "things are getting better," "I feel more energetic," and "I'm pleased with myself." These messages help to maintain a process of positive awareness leading to confidence and self-worth.

If you see this healing process happening in others, it is helpful to offer encouragement without going to extremes of reassurance. Reinforce their tentative positive statements by saying something like, "It pleases me to see you feeling better and looking to the future again." The main reassuring note here is that their faith in the healing process following loss is validated. By personalizing your response with, "It pleases me . . . ," you are giving something of yourself to the other person also. It does not sound so coldly professional.

Being Protective Take precautions, as indicated in the discussion about suicide, in case suicidal thoughts and feelings are entertained or expressed. Weathering this crisis will give you a more solid appreciation of life values. You will have a renewed perspective on your existence after jousting with those fearsome feelings of self-destruction. You also will be in a better position now to use your coping and renewal skills.

Checking Perceptions At this point it is sometimes useful to check your views about grieving. Do you, for example, think that grieving over a loss must be done in a certain way or must take a certain length of time? There are no set norms, but about one-third of people grieving over a severe loss are still grieving after one year. Many grieve for five years, and a few appear to continue the healing process the rest of their lives. There is great variation in the length of the healing process among individuals and among cultural groups. It is important, however, not to compare ourselves to others, but to work on our own timetable that feels comfortable for us.

Cautions About Relapse We want to increase positive statements about ourselves made at this stage, yet we must realize that return to the previous Stage 5 with its depressive feelings and self-defeating behavior also is common.

Knowing about this tendency for relapse could help you prevent it. If relapses happen, you could accept them with calmness and confidence, anticipating that another effort at taking hold might stick.

Explaining relapsing to others after it takes place should reassure them that this is a usual event. The basic idea of growth is that we move ahead two steps and back one, then move ahead again. The healing process described in this book follows this jagged growth line, not the smooth curves in the illustrative figures. Prevention of relapse is a complicated process, but one suggestion that might help is to ask yourself, or the person you are helping, "What action steps do you think you need to prevent lapsing back into depression?" Most people have creative ideas on how they could manage their lives to minimize the probability of relapse.

Discussing the Transitions   Reflections on what happened in this transition, how you responded, and how you are reacting now could lead to productive learning. The key question is, "What did I learn about myself, coping, and transitions through this experience?" It is hoped that these reflections lead to wisdom with which to meet the next life transition with skill, calmness, and confidence. Although it would be useful to do this reflection alone, it probably would be more productive to discuss these learnings with a close friend or professional counselor.

CRITICAL POINT 6: TESTING NEW OPTIONS

Typical Responses

This stage is critical because the growth process described earlier becomes firmly rooted or dies at this point. If healing continues, new energy begins to flow, new possibilities emerge, and hope and optimism spring forth. This means, for example, that you will be thinking about new goals and plans to reach those goals. Expressions such as "Life is more worth living now," "I'm finally out of the pits," and "It is time to move on," will be heard. Of course there will be moments of doubt and lagging courage, but the accelerating power and energy of this stage in the healing process tend to keep it positive and moving.

I suggest that if you can be open to the possibilities of transformational change, you could experience a major shift in your way of looking at the world. For example, you may have felt that your job was merely a grim way to make a living. Now you see that being fired was a blessing and that it created a new opportunity. You begin to see also that work can be a high form of life fulfillment, and that this new job campaign could be the first step in implementing your new view of work and fulfilling life style. If you do not undergo transformational change, there is certainly a very realistic possibility that you will experience renewal change with its new goals, hopes, and plans.

The key tasks of this stage are to keep the growth process going, to avert relapses, and to consider higher levels of functioning and life satisfaction. Once the skills of goal setting and planning become part of your coping repertoire, the growth and renewal process will be self-perpetuating. When you reflect on the learnings about coping style and skills from your recent transition you will join the ranks of hardy copers described earlier—the committed, controlled, and challenged.

Self-Help Strategies and Strategies
for Helping Professionals

Reinforcing Positive Statements   To keep this growth momentum going, it is essential that the emphasis on positive statements continue. You can do this by engaging in positive self-talk like "This feels so good; it's great to look forward again; it is a battle, but I'm winning; I know what I want." In others, listen for their positive self-descriptions, evidence of growing self-esteem, and enthusiasm. The goal is to keep the growth momentum going because seeds of doubt and second thoughts about this scary business of taking hold of new plans and values is there constantly to sabotage good intentions. We need to be wary of well-meaning friends and relatives who sabotage us with comments that often spring from their own needs rather than from consideration for the person in transition.

Another sign of taking hold again is a growing desire to improve performance. The preceding stages have been so characterized by avoidance and inefficiency that any improvement is welcome change. The idea of optimum performance may be attractive to you or the person you are helping. Optimum performance means working up to your potential for achievement and effectiveness. Research on optimal performers by Garfield, for example, resulted in a list of characteristics of optimal performers in entertainment, sports, government, and the professions.[11] Putting aside the talent factor for a moment, let us look at the characteristics of an optimal performer. An optimal performer

- is willing to take risks (to try new activities);
- tolerates ambiguity (can work productively in an environment of confusion);
- has the ability to relax and take time away from work;
- has commitment to essential tasks and challenges but avoids excessive zeal;
- engages in physical activities and renewal efforts;
- is effective in human relations and building support networks;
- practices mental rehearsal of performances;
- challenges popular beliefs;

- focuses energy on tasks and competencies essential for excellence; and
- manages time effectively.

It can be upsetting to compare ourselves with high achievers, but I mention them here to serve as possible goals for working toward your own optimal performance. One approach is to look at your characteristics compared to the preceding list. Do you want to develop more of these qualities? If so, they could be made into goals.

Anchoring Positive Statements *Anchoring* is a term from a counseling theory called *neuro-linguistic programming*, which reinforces statements by touching or by commenting on the positive response.[12] For example, when the other person makes a statement like "I'm going out this afternoon to look for a job," I touch him on the shoulder, smiling, or say something like, "That's great, Jim." The main goal at this stage is to keep the positive statements flowing and the goals increasingly more specific and feasible. A useful activity for yourself is to determine how you are going to anchor your positive self-descriptions. Begin by listing the positive qualities about yourself that you want to retain and strengthen.

Stating Goals Positively and Precisely One task is to make goals specific and realistic. This specificity means that we use precise descriptions like returning to college, taking a trip, or losing a specific amount of weight. We also need broad, general goals that beckon us confidently into the future. Examples are life satisfaction, happiness, purpose, financial security, and loving relationships. We also need some roadmaps in the form of more specific objectives to approach those lofty life goals. You probably recall making new year's resolutions to take off weight or do more exercise; however, these idealistic goals usually foundered on the rocks of vagueness and generality. Right? So the main rule of making good goal statements is to be specific!

Stating goals in positive language helps also. For example, it is more realistic to say "I want to feel better" than to say "I want to stop being depressed." Goals can be even more precise and time-limited through behavior targets. If you want to lose weight, for example, it would be helpful to state your goal something like "I will lose two pounds a week for the next six weeks" instead of "I want to reduce." This goal is modest and achievable. You can actually count the number of pounds lost in six weeks.

Setting goals is only part of the story of self-directed change. Formulating plans for implementing the goals, solving the problem, or changing the behavior is the next step. It is important to have a clear sense of direction for future growth to encourage you to follow through with realistic plans. To summarize, a good goal should be

- stated specifically in behavioral terms;
- time limited, stating when the goal should have been reached;
- measurable so that the extent of the goal achievement can be evaluated;
and
- feasible—that is, realistic for you.

Application Activity: Defining and Analyzing Your Life Goals   Because goals are so important for the renewal form of personal change, it is important to practice setting them. The following application activities will aid you in setting and analyzing your life goals. After completing them, you should have a more clear idea of what you want, what resources you need, and a general timetable and plan for achieving your goals.

Application Activity: Determining What You Want for the Future

To determine your wants, hopes, and aspirations for the future, follow these five steps.

1. List the hopes you have for the outcome of your current transition.

2. List what your aspirations and desires are for an ideal future.

3. Describe the kind of person you want to be in the future.

4. Describe what your night dreams and daydreams are about.

5. Imagine that you are in a helicopter looking down on yourself, your life setting, and your life style five years from now. Describe what you are doing, who the people are around you, and how you are interacting with them at home, at work, and in the community. What are you doing that pleases you and makes you feel good?

Application Activity: Setting Life Goals

Now that you have written down your wants, hopes, aspirations, and desires for the future, translate them into goals and write them in a numbered list. Then renumber the goals to fit your present priorities. Divide your goals into two categories: immediate (the next month) and long-term (the next one to five years). Your list should resemble the following outline:

1. A list of goals for the coming month.

2. A list of goals for the next five years (develop specific time lines and target dates for reaching each goal).

3. A list of specific first steps you plan to take to implement the goal that has the highest priority.

4. A list of long-term considerations for resources (e.g., the time, money, skills, and people that you will need).

Application Activity: Analyzing Goals to Assess the Probability of Achieving Them.

Using the lists you have made, assess the forces working for you in achieving your goals and those working against you. Then you can decide whether to increase the strengths or decrease the obstacles to achieving your goals. You will probably need some of both strategies. Use the following steps to analyze your goals.

1. State your goals. Then, in two separate lists, state the forces pushing you toward your goal (positive forces) and those holding you back (negative forces).

2. Assess and rate the strengths of these positive and negative forces. Rate each force on a scale of 1 to 5 on the relative strength of the force.

3. Decide which positive forces could be strengthened and which negative forces could be weakened to help you achieve your renewal goal.

Involving Your Support Groups The probable missing link in your plan for achieving life goals is awareness that it is difficult to follow through on your wonderful plans. You will find many subtle reasons to sabotage yourself (such as no time, distractions, discouragement, and excuses for delays). List here the special ways you might use to sabotage your goals and plans. This awareness is the first step in eliminating sabotage of your plans.

It is important that other significant people in your life know about your plans and support you. For example, it is useful to solicit feedback on your plans from a member of your support network. Others not only can offer helpful suggestions and lend a supportive ear, they also can help to keep you on track when your motivation lags. For example, you could ask them to call a few weeks into your plan to inquire about how you are doing. They could meet with you periodically to assess progress and give feedback. They could confront you with fantasies about the ways they think you will sabotage yourself. The idea is not to make you dependent on them or to rob you of the thrill of self-directed goal achievement, but merely to arrange conditions so that the probability of achieving your goals increases. In other words, use all available resources to make yourself successful.

NOTES

1 Kobassa, S. (1979). Stressful events, personality, and health: An inquiry into hardiness. *Journal of Personality and Social Psychology, 37,* 1–11.

2 Frankl, V. (1968). *Psychotherapy and existentialism.* New York: Clarion.

3 Silver, R., and Wortman, C. (1980). Coping with undesirable life events. In J. Garber and M. Seligman (Eds.), *Human helplessness: Theory and applications* (pp. 279–375). New York: Academic Press.

4 Kushner, H. (1983). *When bad things happen to good people.* New York: Avon Books.

5 Progoff, I. (1975). *At a journal workshop.* New York: Dialogue House.

6 Gendlin, E. (1978). *Focusing.* New York: Everest House.

7 Frankl, V. (1958, September 13). The search for meaning. *Saturday Review,* 27–36.

  8 Frankl, V. (1962). Basic concepts of logotherapy. *Journal of Existential Psychiatry, 3*, 111–113.

  9 Fugimura, L., Weiss, D., and Cochran, J. (1984). Suicide: Dynamics and implications for counseling. *Journal of Counseling and Development, 63*, 612–615.

  10 Eliot, T. S. (1943). *Little Gidding*. London: Faber and Faber.

  11 Garfield, C. (1980). *Stress and survival*. New York: Mosby.

  12 Bandler, R., and Grinder, J. (1979). *Frogs into princes: Neuro-linguistic programming*. Moab, UT: Real People Press.

Chapter Three

Building Support Systems

WHAT IS SUPPORT?

Gloria has been employed recently by an electronics firm. She is excited and pleased about her new work, but she is fearful and confused by her surroundings. John just lost his mother through death and is feeling sad and alone. Ted has been experiencing many changes in his life recently. These changes have affected his health, and this particular night he is worried and cannot sleep. He wishes he knew someone well enough to call them in the middle of the night to talk. Yvonne has a new child and is having considerable difficulty adjusting to all the changes and new demands in her life. These are a few samples of ordinary life changes for which having supportive people available would make a big difference in how people cope with these changes.

Support is help we receive from friends, relatives, colleagues, and mentors. This support is organized into informal systems called *networks*. Support networking is the act of organizing this support. Networks take many forms, have many advantages, and possess some limitations. They have been helpful to business professionals in the form of "old boy" networks and, more recently, "old girl" networks. These loosely structured and informal groupings are designed to orient new employees to the system and to help with career management and employment transfers. Most budding professionals and business managers regard such support networks as essential to their careers. The research on support is profuse and confirms the common-sense observation that support is essential to mental health and psychological growth.[1]

Often a *mentor*, or informal teacher, is the center of a network. This mentor takes a special interest in the new employee, for example, ensures that the person learns the customs and expectations of the group, and generally acts as helper during the learning phase of the new occupation or job assignment. A *support system* is a network of all the helpers working for the benefit of the person. This chapter describes procedures and skills for establishing such a support system and how to use it to cope with change. This chapter also builds on the common observation that people need other people to survive. In past centuries this need for survival was largely physical and economic. Now it is mainly psychological in the form of nurturance and constructive feedback.

Network *analysis* is a term used by social scientists to describe the function of networks in precise mathematical terms.[2] You will be analyzing your networks, however, in a direct, nontechnical, descriptive manner. The main purpose of this chapter is to provide a simple, yet effective format for analyzing and improving your social support system.

THE PROCESS FOR BUILDING SUPPORT

How is your present support assessed? How can your support networks be changed to make them more useful for coping with change? What skills are needed to build and maintain your support network? A five-step process is presented in this chapter to help you answer your questions about what skills you need and how you can apply them. These steps are as follows:

1 Inventory support people in your network.
2 Assess your various types of support and current levels of satisfaction.
3 Identify and rate the support functions of each support person.
4 Determine changes to be made in your support network.
5 Acquire skills to make the desired changes in your network or in the network of the person you are helping.

Step 1: Inventory Your Network

Inventorying your network involves five tasks:

1 Identify the people in your network.
2 Determine whether you have more than one basic network.
3 Ascertain the intensity or closeness of support for each member.

4 Ascertain the degree of reciprocity of support.
5 Describe your feelings about people in your network.

To identify the people in your network, list all of the people you can recall who are close to you and who are helpful to you in some personally meaningful way. These people will be your close relatives, friends, and associates. This is your primary support network. It may become apparent that there are two or more distinct support groups—one to be called upon for very personal support, such as mourning a loss, and another that might appear to be a business or professional network, which enhances one's career. For example, a young man who was considering moving to a new job in a strange community realized when he did the network analysis that his entire network revolved around his job. His family was not close, and he had no friends away from his work; he depended entirely on his work associates for support. He became aware that after this move he needed to rebuild his network totally, and this time he was determined to diversify that network.

It is possible that your family network operates in opposition to your work-associated network. This condition imposes the necessity of some mediation to reconcile conflicts. Examples are value conflicts around use of leisure time, choice of marriage partners, or use of language. You may finally be faced with a choice of where your loyalties ultimately reside.

An effective way to do your network inventory is to plot a list of people on a sociometric type of diagram, as is illustrated in Figure 3-1. Place yourself in the center, and write the names of people from your list in the circles. This is done in conjunction with task 2—determining whether you have more than one basic network. If there are two or more networks, such as family and personal and business and professional, make two diagrams.

As you apply pencil to paper in locating these supportive people in relationship to yourself, you need to consider task 3—ascertaining the distance and intensity of the relationships. This task is done by drawing arrows from self to the other circles, according to the following suggested guidelines:

- The distance between the self circle and the other circles represents emotional as well as physical distance.
- The size of the circle represents the personal significance of the other person to you.
- Heavy arrows represent close, dependable support.
- Dotted lines represent weak and sporadic support.
- Arrow heads represent the direction of support (one-way or mutual).
- Numbers refer to specific parent, friend, and so forth.

You can see immediately the nature of the hypothetical person's network in Figure 3-1. The spouse is shown, for example, as the person's principal source of support. One child (ch_1) is a weak and distant support, whereas another (ch_2)

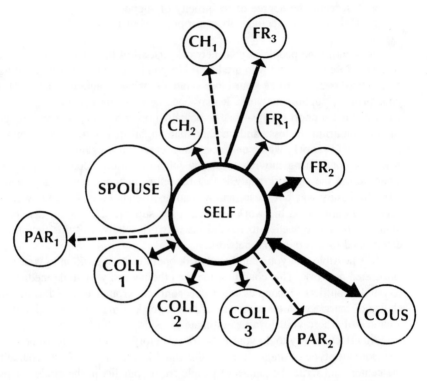

Figure 3-1 Example of a support network diagram. *Note*. The distance between the "self" circle and other circles represents the closeness of the relationship. Heavy lines indicate close, dependable support; light lines indicate modest support; and dotted lines indicate weak support. Arrow heads show whether the support relationship is one-way or mutual. PAR = parents; FR = friend; COLL = colleague; CH = children; COUS = cousin.

is closer and stronger. This person has strong, mutual relationships with three colleagues, and so on.

As you diagram your list of support people, you will become aware of feelings about the people in your support system. For example, you will have warm feelings about nourishing people and perhaps some bad feelings about noxious, demanding people. Some of the relationships you plot will be reciprocal; these relationships will have the double arrowhead. Count the number of reciprocal and nonreciprocal support relationships and record them in the following blanks. Compute your *reciprocity index* as in the following example:

$$\frac{10}{\text{(receive)}} - \frac{5}{\text{(give)}} = \frac{5}{\text{(reciprocity index)}}$$

This index gives you useful information on the balance, or lack thereof, in your relationships with regard to giving and getting. In this example, the person was getting more support from people in his network than he was giving. Whether or not this is a problem depends on your opinions about how much reciprocity should exist in a relationship and how the givers feel about an imbalance. As a temporary condition, a small imbalance is usually not a problem. On the other hand, a large imbalance in either direction would be a problem in the long run because non-reciprocal relationships are difficult to sustain for very long. An example of a highly imbalanced relationship might be a group of family caregivers of an older person. The older adult would probably have a high index of receiving support but would be giving very little. This would usually be an unavoidable and acceptable temporary imbalance, but if a person capable of giving continued to receive a high index, that relationship would be headed for a crisis. Similarly, a high negative index can lead to a crisis for the person who gives much to others but receives little in return. He or she is likely to feel exploited. Even when this person's need to give is strong, he or she eventually resents the continued imbalance.

If you have strong opinions about American social norms of balanced giving and getting, you will have feelings about this issue of reciprocity. Make a note of these feelings, especially about a negative reciprocity index, because they will be valuable data for your decisions later in this analysis of your support network.

So far, you have identified and diagrammed the people in your support network; you have noted your feelings about these people as you placed them on your diagram and as you prepared a reciprocity index. The next step is to identify and rate the specific support functions for each person in your network. In addition, I have defined support as help provided by others, not internal support that we generate ourselves. This internal support is discussed later in the development of cognitive coping skills.

Step 2: Assess Types of Support and Your Satisfaction

Before this activity you probably noted that people in your network perform different support functions. Usually, however, we think narrowly of support as emotional nurturance or "stroking," to put it in popular psychological language. Support comes in many forms, so an important goal is to make support networks satisfy many diverse needs not only for coping with transitions, but also for enriching our lives.

Certainly we need people to make us feel good and to help us through a crisis, but we also need people to challenge us and to give us constructive feedback, even when it hurts. We need people to cry and laugh with us. We also need people that we can call in the middle of the night to discuss some problem or share feelings of sadness, doubt, or joy. There are times when we need expertise or special information. Table 3-1 includes a list of support functions that have been gleaned from research on rating support.[3,4] This list is an extension of the five basic kinds of support cited in the social science literature.

Table 3-1   Assessing Your Support Network and Your Level of Satisfaction

		Ratings of Importance	Ratings on Level of Satisfaction
		This type of support is to me: 1. Very important. 2. Important. 3. Neither important nor unimportant. 4. Unimportant. 5. Very important.	My need for this support: 1. Completely satisfied. 2. Generally satisfied. 3. Neither clearly satisfied nor unsatisfied. 4. Generally unsatisfied. 5. Completely unsatisfied.
1.	*Respectful admiration*	1( ) 2( ) 3( ) 4( ) 5( )	1( ) 2( ) 3( ) 4( ) 5( )
2.	*Satisfaction* pleasures from my contribution to others, joy	1( ) 2( ) 3( ) 4( ) 5( )	1( ) 2( ) 3( ) 4( ) 5( )
3.	*Love* caring, emotional sharing, affection, warmth	1( ) 2( ) 3( ) 4( ) 5( )	1( ) 2( ) 3( ) 4( ) 5( )
4.	*Physical intimacy* touch, sensual pleasure, hugging, sexual satisfaction	1( ) 2( ) 3( ) 4( ) 5( )	1( ) 2( ) 3( ) 4( ) 5( )
5.	*Companionship* sharing, belonging, frienship, laughter	1( ) 2( ) 3( ) 4( ) 5( )	1( ) 2( ) 3( ) 4( ) 5( )
6.	*Encouragement* emotional support, appreciation, expressions of confidence, affirmations	1( ) 2( ) 3( ) 4( ) 5( )	1( ) 2( ) 3( ) 4( ) 5( )
7.	*Acceptance* empathy, understanding, trust	1( ) 2( ) 3( ) 4( ) 5( )	1( ) 2( ) 3( ) 4( ) 5( )
8.	*Comfort* reassurance, forgiveness, someone to lean on or to cry with	1( ) 2( ) 3( ) 4( ) 5( )	1( ) 2( ) 3( ) 4( ) 5( )
9.	*Example* a model, mentor, ideal person	1( ) 2( ) 3( ) 4( ) 5( )	1( ) 2( ) 3( ) 4( ) 5( )
10.	*Direction* advice, direction, spiritual assistance	1( ) 2( ) 3( ) 4( ) 5( )	1( ) 2( ) 3( ) 4( ) 5( )
11.	*Help* material assistance, voluntary helpful activities	1( ) 2( ) 3( ) 4( ) 5( )	1( ) 2( ) 3( ) 4( ) 5( )
12.	*Knowledge* cognitive interactions, expertise, special information and instruction	1( ) 2( ) 3( ) 4( ) 5( )	1( ) 2( ) 3( ) 4( ) 5( )
13.	*Feedback* honest opinions and perspectives	1( ) 2( ) 3( ) 4( ) 5( )	1( ) 2( ) 3( ) 4( ) 5( )
14.	*Other* please specify	1( ) 2( ) 3( ) 4( ) 5( )	1( ) 2( ) 3( ) 4( ) 5( )

Adapted by permission from research conducted by E. Morosan and R. Pearson under the Network for Confluent Development, Inc., Box 874, Belleville, Ontario, Canada.

These are cognitive guidance, emotional support, socializing, tangible assistance, and someone to confide in.[5] These studies showed that disrupting the support network for caregivers of relatives with dementia made those caregivers vulnerable to depression.

To carry out the goals of Step 2, rate your network according to the guidelines in Table 3-1. You are asked to rate each kind of support according to how important that form of support is to you. Note that you are also asked to rate each type of support according to your perceived satisfaction of that need. You may add to the list types of support that you think are missing.

The results will give a more clear picture of the nature and extent of your support, and they will show immediately where the gaps are located. This is not a test, and there are no scores. The purpose is to focus your thinking on types of support and levels of satisfaction. Gaps in your support system should be noted for a later action step.

Step 3: Identify and Rate
the Support Functions Performed

The goal for this step is to identify and analyze the form of support provided by key people in your networks. To reach this goal, you need to

- list key people in your network,
- identify their form of support or behavior that is supportive,
- assess their comparative impact on you, and
- note implications for changing your network.

The first task is to list the key people in your network, as was illustrated in Figure 3-1. Each person performs a key supportive function, and some may perform multiple functions. Examples are provided in Table 3-2. Mary is a very nurturant and friendly person, and her key function is to be an understanding listener. She is available when needed most of the time and lends her understanding ear without showing weariness or boredom. On the chart, Mary's function shows up as "listener."

In the next column of Table 3-2, Mary is given an impact rating on a scale of 1 to 10. Considering the amount and quality of time spent with Mary, she was rated 10 because she was considered a very supportive person. George, a cousin, on the other hand, rated a 1 because he gave very little and took much support. These sample ratings reflect cumulative perceptions of their impact upon the rater. When you complete an analysis of the support people in your life, try to recall your impressions of them in relation to your support goals and needs as identified in Step 2. The purpose is to prepare for Step 4, which is deciding on needed changes.

If you are employed, you may want to construct a special colleague network, because all members serve as talent scouts seeking the best leads for their

Table 3-2 Identifying and Rating the Functions of People in Your Support Network

	Name of Network Member	Form of Support	Impact Rating* 1...5...10 Lo Md Hi	Problems: (Changes Needed)	Changes Planned
Example 1	Close friend Mary	good listener	No problems 10	More reciprocity continue	with Mary
Example 2	Humor, supplies John	office information	Takes too 5	Decrease time much time	by 50%
Example 3	George	Family, emotional support	1	too demanding time and energy doesn't give much	Stop relationship

*Impact is a composite impression based on frequency and quality of contact. The scale ranges from 1 (low impact) to 10 (high impact).

members. The older members serve as mentors and career advisors. Good networks provide introductions to powerful and helpful people in the organization. Networks offer, as a fringe benefit, an informal information service about where to buy, films to see, pending changes, and hot rumors traveling the office grapevine. These networks evolve informally. They are not something one joins, but you might need to consciously nurture a network relationship. A key element is the willingness to give as well as take from the network. It is important also to be visible by attending trade association meetings and conventions, volunteering for committees, and letting your wishes become known.

Step 4: Determining Needed Changes

Some people think this analysis step is a cold, impersonal act that violates the sensitive and loving—even sacred—quality of their support relationships. It appears, for example, that we look at our friends with the attitude of "What's in this relationship for me?" It may seem to focus on what we get rather than on what we give. This criticism is difficult to refute, but we must be aware that we are trying to manage our lives more effectively. The people we contact in the course of living influence us profoundly and affect the quality of our lives greatly. Therefore, it would be prudent to ask ourselves occasionally whether our relationships are helping or hindering not only the quality of our lives, but also the lives of those we are supporting. Furthermore, we do this judging informally when we select or ignore acquaintances as potential friends and when we cull our holiday card lists. So this step involves checking those names on the list of Table 3-2 for possible change of relationship.

Step 5: Making Changes and Acquiring Skills

Planning Changes The last column of Table 3-2 is the space for recording ideas about possible changes in your network that you identified in Step 4. Examples of such changes might be to decrease the amount of time you will be spending with George and to increase the amount of time with Mary. Perhaps you have identified a relative in a distant city who has been serving an important support function for you. You may decide to give this person a call to renew the relationship, or at least assess where it stands at present. The basic reality we need to face in this action step is that our time is finite and, for most of us, very dear. Therefore, we are forced to be selective in the number of people with whom we relate in mutually meaningful ways. Building and sustaining relationships is a very time-consuming activity.

Sustaining Relationships Relationships incur considerable responsibility. Most of us attend to our relationships intuitively and on impulse. Because most of us do not take our relationships lightly, I suggest that we should plan them more purposefully and efficiently. We need to feel a sense of obligation to do our part to nurture those relationships if we want to sustain them.

Expanding Networks Some people lack a support network. They might move or change jobs, thus leaving their networks behind. They might find also that their support is limited to family, or that their friendships are built around their jobs. Thus, an important application for this support network analysis is during a major relocation. A key task, following a move to a new city, the break-up of a family, retirement to a new community, or prolonged confinement in prison, hospital, or overseas assignment is to build a new support network.

Some model programs are in place already to ease these transitions. The American Navy has an extensive program for preparing crews and families for overseas service to reduce culture shock. Businesses that involve the whole family in relocation planning have demonstrated that as a result, relocation is less traumatic. Helping family members to build support through the transition of a divorce has been demonstrated to reduce the stress and trauma of the event. These applications of support networking help to reduce the damaging effects of isolation, culture shock, and mourning that accompany life transitions.

Adapting to Personal Style In assessing your network, it is important to be aware of your basic style of relating. Some of us, for example, feel most fulfilled when we have a large circle of relatives and friends, whereas others of us prefer a small number of people in our networks so we can spend more time with each. Others have many acquaintances with whom they have superficial but occasionally meaningful contacts, and yet their intimates could be counted on one hand. Some people, for example, feel comfortable about seeing their friends once a year at professional meetings, knowing they are available by telephone or letter if a support need arises.

Considering Your Stage in Life Another consideration in preparing for this action step is our developmental stage. Our needs vary with each life stage. In the young adult years, a support network that includes some older adults is useful to provide mentoring functions. Mentors, for example, can help the new employee to learn office procedures and to avoid political pitfalls in the organization.

As people approach middle adulthood, needs for a large circle of close friends may diminish, especially as family ties make those friends less important. In this midlife period, having a few close friends usually is fulfilling enough, although business or professional needs may demand a wide range of acquaintances. In the older years, support groups typically involve family and a few friends for social and recreational pursuits. There are wide individual differences, however, and people must be aware of what they need in the way of support in their stages of life. Then they must give close attention to designing this individualized support system and remodel their present support networks to make them more effective and satisfying.

STRATEGIES FOR MAKING CHANGES
TO ACHIEVE SUPPORT GOALS

Modifying Your Life Style

This action includes joining neighborhood informal support groups where you could meet potential new friends. The list of possibilities is endless, but the main ones are clubs, churches, and special-interest groups. There are groups that cater to singles and couples and to those with specific social and sexual preferences. This strategy of life style modification, however, includes the commitment to spend more time with people, so more than just intention is required. A basic value shift may be involved to enjoy the company of others as much as you prize your time alone. The discussion on setting goals and making plans for change in chapter 2 would help here.

Seeking Mentors

A mentor is a key support person for a young professional. In business settings it is expected that the neophyte manager will have a mentor among the older managers as an aid to advancement and as a model of how to perform successfully. Mentors ensure that their protégés meet the right people, get essential information and advice, and generally act supportively. When these mentoring relationships cross sex lines, however, there may be problems, although research on mentoring problems across sex lines did not disclose any impropriety in the mentoring relationships studied, in spite of popular beliefs to the contrary.[6]

There are some risks in all mentoring relationships. When mentors get in trouble with their superiors, this condition may jeopardize the protégé also. Mary Cunningham, formerly a manager at Bendix Corporation,[7] said that women in particular must consider three guidelines in working with mentors:

- Limit the amount of time spent with the mentor.
- Realize that one is taking some risks, but do it with one's eyes open, especially if the mentor is of the opposite sex.
- Build a power base apart from the mentor.

The general conclusion from writings on mentoring is that mentors are an important part of one's support network, so you might consider building such a relationship with a trusted colleague. Asking for advice or feedback on your performance would be an effective beginning step.

Exploring Available Formal Networks

Some groups exist specifically to provide mutual aid and support. They vary from career groups that are designed to provide business contacts and mutual job-finding assistance, such as the "Over 40" clubs, to special coping groups such as Divorce Lifeline and Alcoholics Anonymous. The basic idea is that these groups are started and run by people who have been through a traumatic life transition such as a divorce or job termination and now are interested in helping others cope with similar life transitions. They usually are called peer support groups because professional helpers are not involved.

Another term used to describe these special networks is *self-support*. That is, they are devoted to the idea that people must depend on their own resources, but that they need a temporary helping hand to steady themselves during the painful phases of their transition. The focus is on learning coping skills that can be used directly in managing the divorce stages, for example. If you are a network member who has the responsibility for making judgments about another person's capability of self-support, there are five key questions to ask:

1   What are the person's present *strengths* (e.g., a strong sense of independence or control of their own lives)?

2   What *resources* does the person have (e.g., finances or friends)?

3   What is the person's *attitude* about receiving help (e.g., open or closed)?

4   To what extent is the person using *available community resources* (e.g., has the elderly person utilized "Senior Information and Assistance" services)?

5   How *capable* is the person of using available resources (e.g., some cannot, or are fearful about, using the telephone or asking anyone for help)?

Part of the strategy for exploring networks is to be aware of available community resources for coping with the crisis stage of the transition, in case one should need such support. Almost all communities now have crisis hotlines, emergency mental health centers, or women's shelters, for example. This resource is considered part of the formal support network. Your informal support network should include people who are knowledgeable about these formal community resources. Part of our responsibility as a member of others' networks is to transmit our special knowledge of how to access these community organizations. The function of many informal support groups—such as those concerned about battered wives, elderly people with disabilities, or abused children—is to compile lists of such formal support groups that can give immediate professional assistance. These groups function much like traditional families offering bonding, intimacy, and sharing opportunities.

Sometimes the right groups are just not available. One strategy is to develop a group that has your desired specifications. This could be a comprehensive helping community or a special support group of close friends that meets at specific times. The American ideal of the hometown or neighborhood served this function in early times. People helped one another—for nursing them through illnesses, raising a barn, or getting in the crops. A spirit of cooperation and caring permeated these communities. "Welcome Wagons" for community newcomers are token efforts in this direction, but you may need a group with more depth and focus. Why not organize one for your specific needs? It is estimated that there are about 600,000 self-help groups in the United States. A clearing house exists to serve as an information center for self-help groups.[8]

If you decide that you want to organize your own support group, you should follow two steps. First, *establish a core group* of people with similar interests that could be the recruiting base for new members. Second, *define the purpose* of the group. There does not need to be formal organization with bylaws and officers; but a minimum of guidelines, such as meeting times and places, are essential to a satisfying group. Such rules should make it easy to join or leave the group.

Informal group norms, such as who chairs the group, or initiates the topics, will evolve with the group. As with all groups, there is a developmental process that follows natural paths. During the affiliation stage, the facilitator or temporary chair arranges introductions, clarifies the roles of leaders and members, and offers suggestions for making the group function. He or she should also realize that later stages involve power struggles, leadership crises, and trust and support problems. Finally, the members need to realize that a *termination stage* is inevitable. Members naturally begin, or need to be encouraged, to seek support outside the group. They also need to become independent as soon as possible so that they can pursue their own lives apart from the group. If you need additional ideas, consult *How to Organize a Self-Help Group.*[9]

Acquiring Skills

Social Skills   After completing the analysis in Step 3, you may become aware that you need some special skill to build your network. Examples are social skills such as introducing oneself or others, or carrying on a conversation during the acquaintanceship phase of a relationship. Many able people feel very shy about these basic skills because they may not have learned them in early years, or they come from a culture in which social skills may be quite different. The obvious solution, if this is your situation, is to take courses or seek tutoring in basic social and conversational skills. Adult education programs of local schools and colleges are good sources. Psychological counselors can provide a setting for role playing social situations and learning social skills.

Assertiveness   Another skill that is often needed to build a desirable network is assertiveness, which means putting yourself forward enough in a relationship to protect your rights and to get what you want. It is often confused with aggressiveness that has anger associated with it. Assertiveness involves a firm and clear statement of your position, opinion, or demand. Classes in assertiveness are offered in adult education programs or sometimes through special programs in women's studies. Much of the popularity of assertiveness training came out of the women's liberation movement, although it is no longer a gender issue. Both men and women need assertive qualities as part of their coping resource kit.

Older adults, especially, need assertive social skills to compensate for their reduced mobility and sensory acuity. Their health problems also limit their ability to get what they want and need in normal ways. A study of older adults with health problems indicated that they are more vulnerable to depression. Having mutually supportive relationships and assertive skills, however, enabled them to get the information and services they needed. This combination reduced their vulnerability to depression, according to research at Purdue.[10]

Curing Boring Behavior All of us need to assess the extent to which we may be inadvertently turning people away by being bores. Buffington looked at the research on boredom and found that bores were characterized by self-centered complaining, triteness (dull conversational subjects), little emotion, tediousness (telling long stories), self-preoccupation, passivity (low contributor), being overly serious (rarely smiles), and being ingratiating (tries too hard to impress and be nice).[11] One of the problems uncovered by these studies is that boring people usually do not know they are boring. They rarely get feedback because being boring is like having bad breath—even your best friends will not tell you.

What is the remedy? Developing the opposite traits to those listed is one approach. Generally, social skills training is needed. Ask your good friends how you come across. "Am I boring?" We can analyze our own behavior and watch the behavior of others. Do they yawn, turn away, flutter their eyelids, and drop their heads? Do you complain a lot? People really are not interested in the details about why your car did not start this morning or about the kids' sore throats. Because conversation is a two-way contract, we need to hold up our end of the contract. Ask questions to involve the other person, but be aware of asking too many questions. Seek the middle ground and be alert to the other person's verbal and nonverbal responses. Finally, for the sake of our own mental health, we need to realize and accept the fact that we are all boring some of the time.

This topic would not be complete without emphasizing the importance of laughter and a general sense of humor. Social networks are nourished by sensible use of humor. Our mental health is enhanced through our ability to see the absurdities, paradoxes, and ironies of life as well as to laugh at ourselves regularly. Cousins's review of health the values of laughter and recitations of his own experience are well known.[12] He discovered that 10 minutes of belly laughter would give him 2 hours of pain-free sleep. It is modern confirmation of the Biblical proverb that "a merry heart doeth good like a medicine."

GENERAL ISSUES IN USING NETWORKS

The underlying assumption that networking support is an effective strategy for prevention of psychological problems is confirmed by research and by common-sense observations.[13] This means that mental health and well-being are enhanced by support networks. There is a prevalent view also that the larger one's circle of friends, the happier one tends to be.

Giving and receiving social support requires heavy commitment in time and energy. Taking this responsibility is often stressful because support has all the positive and negative potential of any human relationship. Giving support has been especially stressful for women who, in their traditional nurturing role, have been vulnerable to feelings of frustration, depression, and depletion when they give and give in a relationship. Furthermore, those on the receiving end of persistent supportive efforts often feel harassed. Sometimes they feel that their privacy has been invaded or that the helper is too eager to find "victims"—subjects for helping efforts. They may be disappointed also that the expected or promised support was not forthcoming. There is general agreement among helping professionals that social networks have the potential for being both supportive and stressful. Therefore, it is important to assess your network accurately and regularly.

The advantages of a dependable support network for coping with change are apparent from the discussion so far. I have emphasized also that it is desirable for support networks to involve reciprocity. There is an American cultural norm that we incur obligations to be supportive to those people in the network who have supported us. Thus, support operates like life insurance. Some people in the network, naturally, will need more attention than others. This condition often results in feelings of resentment in the person who continues to give support but receives little. Eventually the giver feels abused, exploited, and emotionally drained.

An extensive review of research on social support emphasizes the uneven or nonreciprocal nature of much support. Women often take their responsibilities more seriously than do men when involved with common emotional difficulties of people outside the family. Men, for example, tend to minimize a neighbor's illness, but women's caring traditions extend to more concern about the neighbors, thus adding to their strain. Traditional social roles compound the stress also, as is illustrated by the adage "Women make the potato salad and men eat it."

A disadvantage of extended support is the strong possibility of developing dependency in the recipients. Having someone always there to rescue them is likely to reduce their coping capacity in the long run. The child, for example, whose parent is always there to kiss the bumps and ease the pain may not develop the psychological toughness required to survive effectively in a hostile world. Too much support may blunt the strong desire to be independent in adults also. The optimal goal, therefore, is to develop a dependable support system that can be used discriminately in times of need, but that also encourages an independent problem-solving attitude.

Similarly, many support givers need to be aware of their own reluctance to receive support, which they see as dependence on others. This reluctance is not only an obstacle to their receiving needed support, but also it could interfere with giving caring support to others who are perceived as dependent. There is a tendency to project our values and models to others, so this American cultural ideal of the strong, ruggedly independent person may get in the way of giving support to a needy dependent person. The corrective for this possibility is to become more aware of our own attitudes toward dependence and independence and to attempt to modify these views so that we can accept help gracefully.

There are many personal rewards in helping relationships, but much strain often shows while helping others in distress. Caring people naturally empathize with the pain of the other person. Even experienced helping professionals have problems insulating themselves against tensions that spread to the helper. One of the chief innoculators against such stresses is the feeling that one's overtures of support are wanted and appreciated. Most recipients of support express their appreciation, but situations such as caring for a demented parent or a mentally disabled child—neither of whom is likely to be capable of reciprocal response—are very draining on the support person.

A common speculation among helping professionals is that burnout and depression are the costs of maintaining a supportive relationship with low reciprocal rewards. The unspoken give-and-get norm says that if you receive support, you are also expected to give it on occasion. This lack of reciprocity is the source not only of much low-level resentment, but also of anxiety and guilt. This is so especially in families in which the mother sees herself as the chief source of support. Well-intentioned support from grandmothers sometimes is viewed as criticism of a daughter's ability to care for her children or at least is construed as intrusive.

You probably have noted that giving and receiving support requires alertness to potential problems. An important personal goal is to increase awareness of how support affects us and the people we help. A basic caring attitude and interest in people, coupled with a liberal amount of critical self-awareness, goes a long way toward making our efforts to be supportive successful. The following are some ways to reduce the strain of support and prevent the possibility of burnout.

- Change work routines to avoid monotony and renew energy.
- Set new goals, organize new projects, try new ideas, and examine old values.
- Develop a personal relaxation and stress management routine.
- Face honestly the reality of demands against time and energy resources.

• Attend a periodic renewal experience, such as a retreat, workshop, or seminar.

• Balance empathy with detachment.

• Change your job or career, or organize a support group at your work.

• Develop time-out activities, including getaways, holidays, and vacations.

• Maintain self-esteem and physical health as first priorities.

• Conduct a cognitive ecology program to root out negative self-messages.

• Listen to body messages when the strain is getting too much.

• Acknowledge personal vulnerability, and set up a burnout prevention program.

NOTES

1 Gottlieb, B. (1981). *Social networks and social support.* Beverly Hills, CA: Sage.

2 Knoke, D., and Kulinski, J. (1982). *Networking analysis.* New York: Sage.

3 Schumaker, S. (1984). Review of social support. *Journal of Social Issues, 24,* 44–52.

4 Morosan, E., and Pearson, R. (1981, March). Upon whom do you depend: Mapping personal support systems. *Canada's Mental Health,* 1–4.

5 Fiore, J., Becker, J., and Coppel, D. (1983). Social network interactions: A buffer or a stress? *American Journal of Community Psychology, 11,* 423–439.

6 Alleman, E. (1982). *Follow-up report on counselor educators and results of mentoring research.* Unpublished manuscript, Association of Counselor Educators and Supervisors, Falls Church, VA.

7 Cunningham, M. (1984, October 6, interview on NBC television).

8 For information, write to the National Self-Help Clearinghouse, 33 W. 42nd St., Rm. 1227, New York, NY 10036.

9 Humm, A. (1985). *How to organize a self-help group.* New York: National Self-Help Clearinghouse.

10 Altergott, K. (1990, February/March). Coping in times of crisis. *Modern Maturity,* p. 96.

11 Buffington, D. (1990, January). What a bore. *Sky,* pp. 84–87.

12 Cousins, N. (1989, October). Proving the power of laughter. *Psychology Today,* pp. 22–24.

13 Gottlieb, B. (1982). Social support and risk reduction. *Journal of Primary Prevention, 3,* 71–76.

Chapter Four

Changing Thoughts and Solving Problems

Because we are rational as well as emotional beings, we can control our destiny through our thoughts. Most of us do not realize that the majority of our supportive messages come from our own internal thought processes rather than from external sources. We carry on conversations with ourselves each day. This ongoing flow of thoughts, images, memories, and daydreams are called cognitions. Cognitions allow us to remember, decide, and plan without having to enact each of them.

A key coping skill is using our rational capacities to think our way around problems and through transitions. A primary psychological principle is that changing our behavior can start with our thoughts, feelings, or direct action. In this chapter I emphasize how you can change your behavior through your thoughts. The main skills that are discussed are restructuring our thoughts and solving our problems. The focus is on self-managed behavior. This means we assume that we have enormous power over our thoughts and ultimately over our behavior. We do not need outside assistance, except in unusual situations when the transition is especially severe and our emotions are overriding our thoughts.

To illustrate, let us consider a basketball coach having his first losing season in five years. This year a new team from a larger school joined the league and won first place. Because of injuries and missed games, his team finished last this year. His self-talk might proceed as follows: "If I were a good coach, my team would have been on top this year, so it is probably time for me to think about leaving coaching. My team and colleagues have probably lost confidence in me. I'll never be able to recruit good players again." This coach talked himself into a defeatist attitude and a moderate depression. Finally, he said to himself, "I don't have what it takes; I might as well give up." He resigned his coaching job.

In this chapter I describe how we can avoid such self-defeating talk by correcting distortions of the situation and unwarranted self-blame. In this illustration, the coach might see that the record was not due to his personal failure as a coach and that a more reasonable interpretation of the team's record might exist.

APPRAISING THE SITUATION

Research, as illustrated by Pearlin and Schooler's and Lazarus and Folkman's work,[1,2] emphasizes appraisal of the transition. The first step in coping is assessing the situation to decide what strategy is best at this point. Let us assume that you have had a sudden illness that changes your life style. Is the situation life threatening? For example, do you suspect that this change in your health means a drastic alteration in your life style just to stay alive? Is this transition annoying and frustrating? For example, the stressors are causing discomfort, but no imminent threat. Is the transition fairly benign so that you feel little threat or discomfort? If so, ignoring it and letting the healing process take its course would probably be an adequate response. There are three strategies open to you:

- Change the situation.
- Change the meaning of the situation.
- Minimize the personal discomfort (adapt).

If you decide that your health situation is threatening or uncomfortable, then what is the best coping strategy to use? You could change the situation directly by taking medications, submitting to surgery, or altering your habits. You could also neutralize the threat by changing the meaning of the situation. Tell yourself that it is not as serious as first thought or that, compared to five years ago, this is not so bad. This is a strategy of altering our way of thinking about the transition problem in a way that changes the meaning of the problem. Dismissal from your job, for example, could be appraised as a catastrophic problem fraught with many serious consequences. Conversely, dismissal could be thought of as an opportunity to do what you always wanted to do. The next sections of this chapter describe how this coping strategy can be carried out during a transition.

The third strategy, minimizing personal discomfort, is a style of coping that emphasizes acceptance of the situation and not doing anything to change it or ourselves. It focuses on controlling the anxiety through relaxation exercises, medications, or leaving the stressful situation. This strategy is appropriate when the situation apparently cannot be changed or the problem cannot be solved through familiar common-sense approaches. So, we decide that we must live with the situation. An illustration is an older child's announced decision to live at home after living away for some time. The parents interpret this transition event as an intrusion into their privacy. Yet, they do not want to precipitate a crisis or offend their child. They decide to do nothing about it for the time being, and let events take their course. Later, they will use their stress management and cognitive restructuring skills to cope with their anticipated discomfort.

CHANGING NEGATIVE THOUGHTS

The goal of this section is to help you gain skill in using supportive self-talk to help you cope with difficult problems in transitions. Although this is a cognitive skill to be learned, it is important to realize that it has taken many years to develop your present style of self-talk, and this talk is encrusted with layers of emotion. Therefore, you must be patient and persistent to change your patterns of thinking and feeling developed over the years. This skill is called by various names in the psychological literature—for example, correcting negative self-talk, cognitive restructuring, rational therapy, and reframing. I use the term *changing self-talk* in the following discussion. Changing self-talk involves four steps:

1 Be aware of and identify the content of the self-talk.
2 Evaluate the reasonableness of the self-talk.
3 Replace unreasonable self-talk with appropriate self-talk.
4 Practice persistently to change self-talk.

Identifying Self-Talk

The task of becoming aware of self-talk is not easy at first because it has become such a part of ourselves. Self-talk is difficult to comprehend also because it is so habitual and inaudible. You must make deliberate efforts to develop this awareness of your self-talk. Some of the ways are to ask yourself direct questions about what you are thinking in specific situations. For example, habitually ask yourself, "What am I telling myself about this speech coming up soon?" Look at past events and ask, "What did I say to myself before that speech that made it difficult for me?" Look at behavior, such as forgetting an appointment, and ask, "What did I tell myself about this person that would make such an appointment unpleasant?" Then keep a daily record of these thoughts and the associated feelings until it becomes clear how self-talk leads to specific feelings and how it affects your behavior. Recall the basketball coach's sequence of messages to see how this process unfolds.

Another method for facilitating awareness of self-talk is to set aside a regular time of 5 to 10 minutes each week to engage in what Meichenbaum called "cognitive ecology" and what Ellis called "rational–emotive" counseling.[3,4,5] This is a deliberate effort to identify and root out negative self-messages that we have been giving ourselves during the week. We need to look at stressful points, transitions, and unfulfilled expectations. This process of scrutinizing our self-talk is like making a video tape of ourselves and then listening especially to the internal dialogue that goes with the video. Then we evaluate and change our self-talk to clean up our cognitive environment. Examples are thinking that we need to be perfect or competent in all we do; that it is awful and we should be upset when events do not turn out as we hoped or expected; that it is selfish to look after our own interests; that others should always appreciate us for what we are and do; that we must be happy all the time or that other people make us unhappy; and that we should be upset when other people do not behave the way we think they should or that they do not agree with us.

Note the frequent use of *shoulds* and the phrase "all the time" in the messages that upset us. Some of the themes to be especially alert for are the futility of trying to change, comparisons with others, discounting your personal strengths, dire predictions of the future, and impatience with progress. If any of these beliefs or themes match yours, make a note of them for later work.

Application Activity: Identifying Negative Self-Talk

At this point, identify at least four examples of negative self-talk you have experienced in your efforts to adapt to your transition. An example is, "When I retire next month I don't know what I will do with myself." Your examples will be used for applying the evaluations in the next step.

Evaluating Self-Talk

This step takes special effort because we are asking ourselves to admit that perhaps we have been distorting the situation. There are also special emotional reasons for maintaining negative self-talk that are related to our very complicated motivational structures. For example, it is important for some people to be miserable, to feel sad, to punish themselves, and to deny or to distort the feedback of others. You must develop a special willingness to examine your thoughts forthrightly and to be open to the possibilities of changing those thoughts and, ultimately, your behavior.

Assuming that you have jumped over the motivational hurdle just mentioned, it is time to evaluate the reasonableness of your self-talk. Using the videotape analogy cited earlier, imagine that you have a tape of the events involving your self-talk. Imagine a mentor using the questions cited in the following section, while he or she is reviewing this tape with you. The questions are adapted from cognitive psychotherapy principles utilized by Beck in therapy with depressed people.[6] A key characteristic of depressed people is their negative self-talk.

Drawing Unsupported Conclusions Have you drawn a conclusion for which evidence is lacking or for which the evidence supports a contrary conclusion? Referring to the example of the coach, the fact that the coach had won four seasons out of five does not support his being a failure as a coach. To the contrary, evidence supports the belief that he was a successful coach.

Distorting Meaning Have you exaggerated the meaning of the event? For example, have you magnified your problem or its significance? Have you blown up your shortcomings? Have you ignored important information or strengths? For example, the coach disregarded team injuries and the entrance of a team from a larger school into the league. How did these events affect his team's performance? How might these facts have given the coach's self-assessment a more realistic perspective?

Oversimplifying the Situation Are your perceptions of the event oversimplified or rigid? Examples are thinking in absolutes—right/wrong, good/bad, high/low, success/failure—without considering in-between positions. The coach appeared to hold rigid "all or nothing" standards for evaluating his success as a coach—either be on top or be a failure if the team loses. Labeling also is a form of oversimplification, such as the coach's label of himself as a failure.

Overgeneralizing Have you overgeneralized by generating a false conclusion from a single incident? The coach overgeneralized by assuming that one poor season spelled incompetence as a coach. Watch for words such as *always*, *never*, *should*, or *born loser*.

Recall your inventory of self-defeating messages compiled in Step 1. Apply Beck's guidelines to evaluate your self-talk. Where are the distortions in your self-talk?

Replacing Unreasonable Self-Talk with Appropriate Self-Talk

Now that you have evaluated your self-messages, your next step is to restructure them into supportive statements that reflect a more appropriate response to the transition event. The coach might say, "I'm very disappointed that our team lost this year; however, we had some good seasons and we could do better next year. We did the best we could considering the injuries and a new and strong team to compete against. I'll need to take more time to plan an improved strategy for next year." This response faces honestly the feelings of disappointment and resignation about this year, but it also expresses some hope and determination for next year. There is no denial of feelings here, yet there is no unrealistic positive thinking or expectation either. The coach did not say, "We are going to win first in the league next year." The restructuring cognition leads the coach toward realistic and constructive behavior for the preparation and conduct of the next season.

In the earlier illustration of the retiree, he could restructure the pessimism about his pending retirement by saying to himself, "When I retire I'll plan to develop some of my current interests and develop some new ones. I'll probably be plenty busy." He could decide to be a hardy coper and reperceive his retirement as a challenge. You may recall that these hardy copers were expert cognitive reframers who moved from thinking of a transitional change as a catastrophe to thinking of it as a challenge.

In studies of challenge, Maddi and Kobassa and Maddi, Kobassa, and Kahn found that this characteristic also helped to prevent illness,[7,8] Furthermore, they claimed that this trait could be acquired or strengthened through training in what they called "situational reconstruction," which is very much like the cognitive restructuring described earlier. Trainees reviewed their stress-producing experiences in a broad perspective, imagined the worst possible scenarios, and then planned alternative courses of action to reduce the likelihood of those scenarios actually happening.

Application Activity: Change Negative Self-Talk

Select one of the four statements you identified in the first step and restructure it to reflect a more positive view toward your transition. Try to avoid making overly optimistic restructures or being excessively cautious. For example, if you have had a transition involving a change in relationship, you might say, "Although it will be difficult leaving this relationship, I'll probably have opportunities again in the future. I am an attractive person, and I relate well to people." This statement acknowledges the difficulty of leaving; it puts new relationships in the realm of possibility; it has reasonably optimistic expectations; and it affirms positive traits. This kind of statement differs from a Pollyanna type of positive thinking, by which people tend to make rosy predictions, possibly leading to further disappointment and disillusionment. This view recognizes that we cannot always have the world the way we want it. An example of excessive optimism is, "Everything is going to turn out real cool. My new boyfriend is just around the corner looking for me."

Practicing Changing Self-Talk

After you have become aware of the content of your self-talk (Step 1) and evaluated the reasonableness of your own self-talk (Step 2), you can begin to replace unreasonable self-talk with more appropriate self-talk (Step 3). To become adept at changing negative or unreasonable self-talk, however, requires persistent practice. The ultimate goal of changing self-talk is to change your behavior. In the following section I discuss some strategies that you can use to transform self-talk into action.

STRATEGIES FOR CHANGING BEHAVIOR

Questioning Basic Assumptions and Beliefs

During traumatic transitions, our basic assumptions about the world often are shattered. Each of us has a personal view of reality to make sense out of an otherwise chaotic world. These views are tightly held assumptions about the world and of ourselves in relation to it. These assumptions and learned beliefs guide our actions. We are seldom aware of these basic guiding principles until some event, such as a transition, takes place that challenges or upsets our world view. Some examples of these assumptions, cited by Janoff-Bulman,[9] are that we are invulnerable, that the world is just and comprehensible, and that we are basically virtuous. When a severe transitional change takes place, our world is no longer comprehensible and we feel out of place, unstable, unbalanced, and insecure.

When we are in a transition we need to reaffirm our assumptions and alter them so they are more functional or replace them. The assumption of invulnerability is expressed as "It can't happen to me." As a protective device, we humans have a tendency to overestimate the possibility of experiencing positive events and underestimating the likelihood of negative events.[10] Examples are views toward becoming a victim of crime, accident, earthquake, or disease. We maintain the illusion that we will not be a victim by continuing to smoke, drive without seat belts, and walk dangerous streets. This protected view is maladaptive only when we ignore threatening actions or it causes us to act in a foolhardy manner.

When we have an accident or are robbed, the illusion of invulnerability is shattered and it may result in feelings of helplessness and panic. There are also fears of recurrence of the event. What is even more distressing is the decline of trust and the feeling of insecurity, especially when associating with other people. This broken trust relationship becomes a force for changing our beliefs about invulnerability and safety.[11] The assumption that the world is meaningful, orderly, and understandable comes into question also during severe transition experiences. Our world is no longer predictable and controllable, so we become more fearful and cautious.

Another assumption is that the world is populated by good people and that we are protected against misfortunes by this fundamental goodness in people. A corollary of the just world view is that people get what they deserve. When misfortune hits, especially a criminal act, our assumptions about our virtue protecting us are shattered again. The world does not make sense when good people are victimized. One unfortunate consequence of such events is that people begin to see themselves as flawed, weak, helpless, and out of control. Perceptions of self-worth and confidence also decline.

People with a theistic world view perceive themselves as special creations under the protection and nurturance of a benevolent God. They assume that as long as they maintain this relationship to God they will be afforded special comfort when severe transitions take place. For many people this belief system offers considerable support during critical times of the transition; but others feel abandoned, confused, and punished by the transition event. Some experience disillusionment and dissolution of their faith in divine intervention and prevention.

Changing World Views and Beliefs

What can be done to help ourselves and other victims whose basic views of the world are crumbling? Changing self-talk is a key to redesigning our assumptive world. We can admit to our vulnerability and attest that we may have had an unrealistic view of events and people. We need to restructure them into more palatable and useful assumptions. Concentration camp victims are extreme examples of how people had to find some meaning to their existence apart from the appalling conditions of the camps. Crime victims need to see their experience in terms of the probability of events, such as being at the wrong place at the wrong time. Bad things happen to good people without any personal intervention on their part.

People must realize that much time is needed to recover from their shattered beliefs, but they also must attempt reconstruction of a new set. One caution in this reconstructive task is to avoid going to the extreme of perceiving the world as a wholly malevolent place and to look upon destructive transitions as primarily random events. The goal is to reconstruct a reasonable self-image of worth, dignity, autonomy, and power. The person should not be alarmed by the persistent intrusive thoughts of the traumatic transitional event; time is necessary for the healing process to take effect. It also takes time for the new assumptions to fit with the new experiences. In summary, the task of reassessing our belief systems is completed when the transition event is redefined and accepted emotionally, and when we have rationally analyzed the extent of our personal responsibility for the transition.

Additional coping attitudes that help in redefining beliefs and reframing experiences are comparing ourselves to others less fortunate, admitting that things could be much worse, and perceiving some benefit (such as personal growth) from the event. For example, the hostages at the American Embassy in Iran universally felt that the experience made them stronger people. Seeing meaning in the event, such as being an innocent hostage, also helped the redefining process.

In addition to redefining meaning of the event, some direct self-attributions of beliefs are helpful in coping. For example, we must believe strongly that we have the power to change our life circumstances—that we are not victims of whimsical forces of fate. If we look at the development of human society over the centuries, it is apparent how we have achieved increased control of our environment and consequent predictability in our lives. Underlying this increased personal power is the conviction that we can make an impact and that we are important change agents.

A related belief that warrants consideration is that we are a part of the problem. Problems usually do not just spring out of trees and attack us. They are complex events over which we usually have some control. We must also believe that although a desire for change and personal effort are important preconditions for personal growth, it takes more than willpower to effect lasting change. We must be aware that there is a technology and a group of skills about change that can be learned. Finally, we must develop some perspective on pain and suffering. It is important to view suffering, such as depression, as a signal that something is wrong in our lives, just as a fever signals illness in the physical domain. Suffering has survival value as we experience losses in life transitions and realize that the stress of change is inevitable.

In transitions we are frequently confronted by issues around the difficulties of living life as we want it. So much of Western culture focuses on easing the pain of personal problems. We spend so much time and effort escaping pain and suffering through drugs (both legal and illegal), compulsive pleasure seeking, and excessive work addictions at worst or complaining and whimpering at best. It is natural to seek happiness and certainly relief from pain, but finding a balance between the extremes of escapism and fatalism (a tragic view of life) on the one hand and an optimistic and euphoric view of life (emphasizing life's opportunities and pleasures) on the other hand is difficult to strike. After a painful transition it is understandable why some people's tragic view of life is reinforced, and why a balanced view that life is full of both pain and joy is elusive.

One solution to this value dilemma is to perceive and accept life as realistically as possible. This means perceiving living as a difficult and frustrating endeavor. This is a theme of Peck's book *The Road Less Traveled*, which was on the New York Times' best seller list for six years.[12] That life means suffering is an old idea that is emphasized in the Bible and in Buddhist writings. Jung wrote that neuroses are always substitutes for legitimate suffering and can be eased only when the substitute neurosis becomes more painful than the original legitimate suffering.[13] Peck emphasized that this process can be reversed by facing the realities of life with courage and discipline so that one can reexperience legitimate and normal human suffering. He suggested four approaches to this self-discipline:

- delayed gratification, or the capacity to postpone pleasures (e.g., do difficult tasks first and save the pleasurable ones for last);
- accept responsibility (e.g., face problems rather than avoid them);
- dedication to truth (e.g., rigorous self-examination and self-honesty and being open to challenge and willing to admit error); and
- balance (e.g., attempt flexibility on major issues as in expressing anger, exerting control, and self-expression—like giving up freedom of speed for control and safety in a speeding car).

Thought Stopping

Our beliefs and ways of thinking have developed and have been reinforced over a lifetime. So, they are not changed easily. Cognitive restructuring skill requires continual practice. When these restructuring efforts falter there is a "fall-back" method called thought stopping. As the name suggests, this is deliberate interference with the idea in our thinking process. Thought stopping is done by saying to yourself "Stop!" For example, if you find yourself persistently thinking self-defeating thoughts you say to yourself "stop that" very emphatically.

The value of this method is that it interferes with the automatic thinking that gives us trouble. It opens more possibilities for developing positive self-evaluations, for example, to replace negative self-evaluations. For a more physical aid to thought stopping you could have a rubber band on your wrist during the day. When an unwanted thought persists you can snap the band when you say "stop."

Affirming Strengths

A useful antidote to negative self-evaluation is to compile a list of your strengths and assets. As you write them, savor and prolong the good feeling generated by this list of strengths. Sort them by your various roles, such as work, family, civic, and friendship. Note the clustering of your lists under your roles. What implications for developing more strengths for a particular role, such as father, are apparent? These strengths are very affirming qualities and make us feel good about ourselves.

Taking Effective Action

The examples so far of assumptions and beliefs that need reconstruction are mainly in the cognitive realm—that is, changed by altering our thinking about them. These altered thoughts suggest appropriate action. For example, the jilted lover must actively seek new relationships. The retiree must develop new interests. The victim of an assault not only must change cognitions about vulnerability and safety, but also must act more constructively. Examples are installing security systems after a burglary, learning self-defense, or changing a residence or telephone number. The terminally ill person must assume more responsibility for self-care.

As in all transitional events, seeking the support of significant people is an effective action. If you tap your support network, do not be unexpectedly distressed if some of your friends do not respond as warmly as you would like. Many people feel uncomfortable talking with people who are in pain. They have some assumptions about victims and "unacceptable" pain that intrude on their helping efforts. For example, they may see you as responsible for your plight, as a loser, or as a person to be avoided to escape feeling your pain.

One common trap to avoid is blaming others or yourself for the transition. Human service professionals are divided over the value of self-blame. On the one hand, some say that a little self-blame is an effective antidote to denial. On the other hand, some claim that it is a maladaptive personal style and a sign of depression. So, there may be two types of self-blame. Constructive self-blame may be characterized in self-talk such as "I should not have attempted to walk down that dark street so late at night." The focus is on the responsible behavior of the person; as a result one could be in a better position to avoid future victimizations. People who exhibit maladaptive self-blame may think of themselves as bad people with character defects who deserve to be victimized. The first type, or behavioral self-blamer, would find it easier to reconstruct a more meaningful world and get on with living, whereas the characterological self-blamer would be persistently wondering "Why me?" or saying to him- or herself, "poor me," and "What a bad person I am."

Let us assume your goal is to feel better. You have been feeling blue too long. The first task is to break that big goal of feeling better into smaller steps. These steps are illustrated in Table 4-1 and summarized as follows.

1 Describe the problems or tasks.
2 Determine specific target behaviors (goals).
3 Collect information about present behavior.
4 Apply a method leading to change and record results.
5 Evaluate results or progress toward the target (goals).
6 Reward positive results to provide continuity of the new behavior.

To return to the illustration of wanting to feel better during the painful transition—the first step, after perceiving the problem as pain and discomfort from the transition, is to determine what needs to be done to make you feel better. These are called target behaviors. They are specific things that you must do that will lead to the consequence of feeling better. What do you think are some of these behaviors associated with depression that could be changed?

Some additional answers you may have to this question are self-critical put-downs, reduced activity level, low energy, and no pleasurable activity. Note that

Table 4-1 Process of Self-Managed Behavior Change

1. Describe the problem (state goal)	2. Determine target behavior (increase or decrease)	3. Observe and record present behavior (how much? how often?)	4. Apply skills to change behavior (record results of skills)	5. Evaluate progress (results for target behavior)	6. Reward positive results
I feel depressed now.	1. Increase self-affirmations 50% in one week.	1. Two affirmations per week; 12 negative statements per week.	1. Cognitive restructuring twice a day. 1. Daily affirmations.	1. 25% increase in positive affirmations.	1. I like myself better.
I put myself down consistently.	2. Eliminate discussion of my depression with friends.	2. Two discussions with friends about depression.	1. Thought-stopping when thinking of depression. 2. Conversations on nondepressive topics.	2. No discussions of depression with friends.	2. I'm having more fun.
I have no pleasurable activities.	3. Engage in 5 pleasurable activities in the next week.	3. No pleasurable activity.	3. Go swimming two times a week. 3. Go to the hairdresser.	3. Started three activities: swimming twice, out to dinner once, had hair set.	3. I'm making progress.
My goal is to feel better.					

the goal is to feel better, not to reduce the depression. You must decide which target behaviors you will list after the problem description and goal in Table 4-1. Then you must decide whether this target behavior should be increased or decreased. For example, self-criticism needs to decrease, pleasurable activity needs to increase. Note from the example in Table 4-1 that the target is very specific in terms of percent of increase in one week. This gives you some specific ideas on progress toward your target. You have probably noted that this method is similar to the goal-directed process described earlier, except that now the process is directed toward changing a problem behavior.

To enhance your motivation for this self-change activity I suggest that you ask yourself how your life will be affected if you change your target behavior. In other words, what are the gains and losses? List the consequences systematically as desirable things you would gain and lose and as undesirable things you would gain or lose. You can be more confident when you see that the list of desirable consequences is much longer than the list of undesirable consequences.

The next step is to collect information about how often you give yourself a put-down or a self-affirmation in a week or a day. This gives you a baseline for deciding whether you are making progress. Then a specific skill is applied to make the change, such as thought stopping or going to the hairdresser. Finally, after a set period such as a week, you ask yourself how you progressed. Did you meet your target? If not, why not? Did you give it your best effort? Was the target too high or too low? Then adjust the target for the second week, and so on. This periodic review gives you clear feedback on how you are going, and if it is in the direction you desire, it gives you a tremendous boost. You see that you are making progress under your own efforts.

A principle from behavioral technology that applies throughout this process is *reinforcement*. This is a frequent reward—preferably an internal one from your own feelings of satisfaction. Rewarded activities, especially those administered on a fixed or intermittent schedule, tend to be repeated. Sometimes it is difficult to get the specific behavioral result you want, such as honest self-affirmations. Therefore, you must *shape* your behavior by finding anything in your daily activity that warrants self-praise. Reward it and similar activities that are close to vigorous self-affirmations until you get the full effect you want.

A related idea is that of *antecedents*—cues that tell you what behaviors are appropriate for a situation. A road sign tells you what behavior to perform, for example. An important implication for self-managed behavior is to look at the cues that trigger our behaviors and then focus on changing those cues. If we are trying to lose weight, for example, we will put the ice cream carton in back of the fruit or get rid of it altogether.

Eliminating behavior we do not want can be aided by the *extinction* process also. This means not rewarding the behavior until it gradually dies out from lack of reinforcement. For example, demanding behavior from others can be reduced by ignoring the demands. Sometimes the behavior change principles can be used in combination. For example, you may wish to extinguish the demanding behavior through extinction and then shape the behavior you want by rewarding requests and suggestions.

Another important behavioral principle is *modeling*. When we want to change our behavior it helps to find someone who is a good example of this behavior and then copy it. For example, if you want to acquire more confidence, you look for someone who acts confidently. Observe and associate with this person, focusing on how you can be more like that person.

Application Activity: Charting a Behavior Change Plan

Using the principles and illustration described in this section, choose at least one target behavior and fill in a chart as in Table 4-1. It will take practice to get over the feeling of awkwardness in doing an exercise such as this. The goal is to make the self-managed behavior change process a part of your problem-solving routine so that it becomes a natural skill for you. To become more informed on self-managed change, I suggest you read special books on this topic by Mahoney, Thoreson and Mahoney, and Bernhard.[14,15,16]

PROBLEM SOLVING

Self-managed behavior change is one approach to solving personal problems when the goal is to change a specific undesired behavior. Most problems in transitions, however, are more general and undefined. For example, the methods of solving problems that I discuss in this section are applicable to questions such as, "What will I do when I retire?" "How can I face this divorce?" "Should I change jobs now?" "How can we best plan this move?" The goal of this section is to develop problem-solving effectiveness. This means the ability to choose and use the most appropriate strategy of problem solving from a menu of approaches. Research studies indicate that adults have a favored problem-solving strategy, but they are not flexible in their choice of response.[17,18] In other words, they tend to use the same method for all types of problems.

Personal feelings of power or powerlessness also affect choice of problem-solving strategy. If people believe they are powerless to change themselves or their situation, they are more likely to develop a fatalistic attitude of "what's the use?" Thus, a first step in any problem situation is to gain awareness of how you feel about yourself in problem situations. The second step in awareness is to realize that rather than doing nothing or throwing yourself emotionally at the problem, you can choose a strategy suited to your style and situation.

There is little research to indicate exactly how to make this choice of appropriate styles, but there is sufficient information about the different styles of problem solving and their teachable subskills to proceed with confidence. I present three common styles of problem solving and their component skills so you an apply them selectively to your transition problem: trial and error, linear or logical, and intuitive or creative.

Trial and Error Style

Trial and error is the most common method of solving problems. It begins with awareness of what the problem is about. Then the person applies his or her experience to attempts at solutions until one fits. The discovered solution is a rewarding condition, so the next time a similar problem presents itself the person will attempt to use the same approach. This is the common method of problem solving by the more intelligent animals, but as a human problem-solving strategy it has many weaknesses. Its only strength is that it is a type of common-sense approach to problems when past experience is the guide. This is why it is called a "reproductive" rather than a "productive" strategy.[19] An example is solving a cube puzzle by successively trying different approaches until one stumbles on a solution. Then, the next time one is faced with such a task, the solution is tried. This style is sometimes called "learning by experience," or less flatteringly as "muddling through." Two other styles—linear or logical and creative or intuitive—are recommended for your kit of coping skills because they are more effective and cover a wider range of problem situations.

Linear or Logical Style

The linear style is systematic and logical. Information is used extensively. Computers are a considerable aid in processing this information. I want to offer a precautionary note here because of the contradiction between a logical and systematic approach to solving problems and real life. Real life problems in transitions are so complex, changeable, and intermittent that a logical process often appears out of keeping with reality. In addition, problems come in multiples and have various solutions, so it is difficult to evaluate when the problem is "solved." The following steps, therefore, should be considered as guidelines for thinking through problems. They are guidelines rather than a rigid formula for the way people really solve personal problems. It is my firm opinion, however, that the following steps could serve to clear up much of our illogical and ineffective problem solving. In addition, these steps help to separate the thoughtful problem solving from the associated emotions, such as fear and anger, that usually are present. These sequential steps are as follows:

1 Becoming aware of the problem.
2 Stating the problem.
3 Formulating goals.
4 Generating alternatives.
5 Collecting data.
6 Deciding among alternatives.

7 Provisionally trying out an alternative.
8 Evaluating the solution.
9 Selecting an alternative solution if necessary.

Becoming Aware of the Problem   A crucial preliminary step in all problem solving is to be aware of the nature of the problem. An example of a self-message is "I have a problem that I need to work on." This point seems obvious; yet, denial is at work so often when problems swirl around us. We often do not even want to admit that there is a problem, so avoidance is a common response. An example is the man who starts drinking alcohol during his transition to the extent that it affects his mental and physical functions. Yet, he denies that his drinking is excessive.

Part of problem awareness is to decide who "owns" the problem. A mother, for example, says to her daughter, "I think you had better get some counseling." The daughter says she sees no need for counseling. The mother is even more upset. It appears that the mother has the problem for the present time.

This first step of admitting the presence of a problem is important also in making the decision whether the linear or intuitive style would be better in this instance. Sometimes, focusing on problem awareness reveals that there really is no problem. Occasionally, when confronted by awareness of a very difficult problem, some people become anxious and express doubts that they have the capability to solve the problem.

It is important at this early step to develop a workable "problem set," which means a readiness and confidence to more toward a solution. It also means developing a realistic view of the problem—neither minimizing its complexity nor exaggerating its importance. It may be necessary, for example, to apply the cognitive restructuring methods described earlier when messages creep up, such as "I can't solve this problem" or "I feel overwhelmed by it all. I just want to run away and crawl into a barrel."

Stating the Problem   This step is an effort to make a clear statement of the nature of the problem. A clear problem statement looks very much like the goal statement cited in the earlier discussion of planning and goal setting. A problem statement contrasts where we are now (confusion, pain, stress) with where we want to be (the desired solution and resolution). Often, going through the process of problem definition leads to a more clear awareness of possible solutions. Clear problem definition usually deters impulsive and premature jumping toward solutions. H. L. Mencken is alleged to have said that there is always an easy solution to every human problem—neat, plausible, and wrong.

Four questions must be answered in writing a problem statement:

- What kind of problem is it?
- Who is affected?

- Who is causing it?
- What is the goal?

If a couple in the transitional problems of a divorce says, "We have a communication problem," this statement assumes that there is a discrepancy between the present confused situation and the way the couple wants their marriage to be. Their phrase "a communication problem" is not specific enough as a problem statement. The couple then elaborates their problem statement as "We need to discuss our feelings about each other more, including talks with the children." Note that the people affected are included in the problem statement. The question of who is causing the problem is stated as "we" who need to discuss. The immediate goal is to increase shared feelings, and the ultimate goal is to decide the future of the relationship. It is crucial in this analysis of the problem to identify the key element. For example, is it a lack of clarity, disagreement, lack of skill, lack of resources, too little or too much communication, insufficient time, conflict over decisions, a power struggle, or expression of inappropriate feelings?

Formulating Goals After a clear statement of the problem, it is time to think of translating the problem statement into a goal statement. What does the couple want their relationship to be in the future? They have initiated divorce proceedings but feel conflict about this impulsive decision. Their goal, therefore, is stated as "We want to discuss our feelings more openly and clearly so that we can decide in a month whether we can maintain this relationship or whether we should separate."

Generating Alternatives The couple must sit down and calmly discuss their various possibilities for action. They can consult with a marriage counselor; they can have a family conference. They can try living apart for a few weeks, and so on. By this kind of brainstorming of alternative courses of action to solve their problem (or reach their goal), they can see the whole range of possibilities before them.

After selecting the most feasible and attractive alternatives from the list, a force field analysis can be initiated. This method was described in chapter 2 and is adapted here for problem solving. On the top of a sheet of paper, write the alternative action chosen to analyze. Let us assume it is the consultation with a marriage counselor. Place a vertical line in the middle. In the left column the couple writes all the reasons they can think of for consulting a marriage counselor. These are forces pushing them toward the consultations. In the right column they list the reasons for not seeing a counselor. These are the forces restraining them. This process helps to clarify the strengths of the pro and con forces for this action alternative. Usually this analysis, along with gathering relevant information, clarifies the various possibilities for action so that choosing among the alternatives are easier.

Deciding Among Alternatives   Usually, after going through the problem definition and analysis process, the most desirable alternative stands out. There is a feeling of comfort and confidence about the choice. Sometimes the alternative is not clear, or there are several equally attractive, unattractive, or conflicting alternatives. In such situations an arbitrary decision is made on the basis of feelings of "rightness" about the choice. When moving to the next step, the provisional try, the couple cited earlier realizes that this is a tryout and that other alternatives can be tried after evaluating the effectiveness of this one.

Trying Out an Alternative   The next step is to try the chosen alternative. Then the outcomes of the choice are evaluated. Let us assume that the couple chooses to see a marriage counselor. After three sessions they share opinions about whether this counseling has moved them toward their goal of clarifying the direction of their relationship (evaluation). If their decision is that the counseling alternative has not moved them toward their goal, they discuss trying another alternative.

On the surface, this kind of process appears laborious, but there are two advantages over the trial and error approach. It prevents impulsive and precipitous action, where the couple might have moved from a vaguely defined problem of "we have difficulties with communication" to action—"we must initiate a divorce." Vaguely defined problems beg for instant solutions because they make us so uncomfortable. A premature jump from problem statement to solution often leads to additional feelings of failure, frustration, and uncertainty. Second, logical or linear problem solving separates the rational process of decision making from the strong feelings associated with the action. Certainly, feelings are important data to consider, especially in a critical decision such as divorce, but it is desirable to keep them in perspective during the problem-solving process. Third, the solution is regarded as provisional tryout with continuous monitoring and comparison with facts and observations. This approach reduces rigidity and a feeling of being locked into a solution.

Evaluating the Solution   The key question to be answered at this step is how closely does the chosen alternative match the goal cited in step 3? If it is close the problem is considered solved. If not, an additional step of selecting an alternative solution is undertaken. The evaluation step, of course, is repeated and additional information is collected to assess the adequacy of the problem-solving process.

Application Activity:
Using a Linear Problem-Solving Style

Recall a personal problem that you have worked on recently. What steps did you go through? How effective was your process? How did it differ from the process just described? Choose a problem that you are facing now or plan to face in the near future. Keep in mind the broad definition of a problem. Choose a personal situation that you do not like, that you wish would be different, and that you are uncertain as to how to achieve a solution.

What difficulties did you have in working through the nine problem-solving steps? Was the logical or linear style appropriate to your problem? How did you adapt this process to your problem? What did you learn about your problem-solving style? If your problems appear to be too complex or confusing for self-solution, I suggest you confer with a friend or a psychological counselor who thinks in terms of helping people solve problems. Perhaps you need to think about how you can divide your problem into subproblems. Some suggestions for further reading on personal problem solving are books by Dixon and Glover and by Adams.[20,21,22].

Intuitive or Creative Style

Intuitions are characterized by vague body sensations and hunches that have little foundation in fact or logic. Intuitions are ways of knowing without knowing much about how we know. Often intuitive solutions are risky leaps into the unknown. Sometimes intuitive styles appear to have spiritual, or at least mystical, connections. As a result, problem-solving approaches using these ideas appear to be soft from a cognitive and behavioral perspective. Intuitive approaches have a long history, however, and in many parts of the world it is the preferred approach to solving personal problems. The task of psychological research is to ascertain which human problems best match which style of problem solving in particular cultural settings. In my view, the intuitive approach is a valuable resource to complement and enhance the linear styles. Physicians, scientists, and judges admit to using intuitive judgments in solving their professional problems.[23]

The intuitive style has teachable skills and attitudes, although they are not precise enough to learn directly. Preferences and talent for the intuitive style may be related to brain hemisphere development. The right brain–left brain research is not sufficiently developed to have precise practical applications at present.[24] Terms such as *incubation, illumination,* and *insight* are difficult to define. The purpose of this section is to examine some of the underlying beliefs and assumptions, as well as some of the procedures and applications, of the intuitive style.

Beliefs and Assumptions   The essential set for successful intuitive or creative problem solving is a general receptivity to new ideas. Because the thinking process is novel and unconventional, openness or a lack of rigidity in content and method is necessary. Patience and submission are key virtues because, paradoxically, often the more aggressive the search for a solution, the more elusive that solution becomes. Saturation in the subject and having a huge factual background in the problem are helpful. Contrary to popular belief, it helps to have a background of information and experience to build upon in the problem area, although past experience can be an obstacle if used for justification of present beliefs and actions.

We must ask questions from many perspectives because solutions are often limited by the way the questions were asked. After questioning and a lengthy period of contemplation about the problem (incubation), the solution often appears in awareness. The receptivity and incubation processes are helped by relaxation, visualization, and concentration. Finally, intuitive problem solving is enhanced by a basic trust in the wisdom of the body. Sometimes we call this physiological and sensory emotional data "organismic wisdom."

Process   There is no standard set of procedures or steps in the intuitive style. It is nonlinear, and solutions seem to appear spontaneously in the presence of certain conditions. The attitudinal set just described is a start. The following list contains some of the conditions that facilitate intuitive or creative problem solving.

- Physical relaxation.
- Incubation time.
- Contemplation of problem elements.
- Focusing on bodily experience.
- Imagery.

Basic Conditions for Intuitive Problem Solving   The initial facilitative condition is a state of deep physical relaxation. This relaxed condition generates a mental state of receptiveness, openness to ideas, hunches, and extrasensory perceptions. The precise methods of achieving this relaxed state and receptiveness are described in the next chapter.

Incubation time is needed to mull over the problem, review past experiences with the problem, and project possible alternative solutions. It is a time to make sure that the questions being asked are the most important and productive ones. To the external observer there may not seem to be much going on, but during the incubation period there is much creative thought about possibilities for redefining the problem, asking alternative questions, managing ways of processing information, and relating possible alternatives to possible solutions.

Pirsig, in *Zen and the Art of Motorcycle Maintenance*, described an intuitive form of problem solving.[25] He emphasized that the incubation process is a long period of silent staring at the broken machine. This contemplative stance allows time to shed old opinions about what might be wrong. He also avoided impulsive actions that might further damage the cycle, and he was less likely to overlook solutions that were not apparent on the first inspection. It is a process of blending with the machine—of *being* that cycle for a while.

Pirsig emphasized the importance of motivation, or determination. He called it "gumption." This motivating thrust to solve the problem can be eroded by external conditions, such as illness or severe personal problems. Another gumption trap is the rigidity of thought that comes from overconfidence and arrogance about knowing the correct solution.[26,27] The technique of the monkey trappers cited in chapter 2 illustrates this problem. The monkeys' rigid focus on food retention blocked out solutions to the problem of how to escape capture.

Experiential Focusing   This is a process of attending to the felt bodily experience of a problem. This method assumes that more cognitive attempts have been ineffective for the type of problem at hand, which is likely to be vague and to have elusive solutions. Gendlin has developed a procedure for focusing that is useful in intuitive problem solving.[28] One characteristic of Gendlin's procedure is that it consists of a sequence of activities emphasizing awareness of bodily processes. The assumption is that we have the solutions to many of our problems in our organismic wisdom. The task, then, is how to access this wisdom to solve our personal problems.

In the first phase, the person with a vague problem is asked to describe his or her body experience (e.g., tense or relaxed). Then the person is asked to describe feelings experienced now in their bodies. This experience is followed by a statement of awareness about why these experiences are being felt at this time. The problem solver is then asked to focus on "a felt sense" and what the problem feels like in the body. This is the known part of the problem. There is a shift in awareness from the known sensation to the unknown, called "about-ness." Again, attending to sensations and gently asking the person what they are about generates images and words that match these sensations. The test of appropriate aboutness that leads to solutions is emotional release and relaxation when these new images are verbalized. It just feels right. Receptiveness is important here because listening to, rather than talking to, one's body is the key. The focusing process continues to other images that may emerge from experience.

What happens when the problem defies solution? If a solution is earnestly desired, but the person appears to be stuck, the focus should shift to the bodily experience of being stuck. This helps to overcome the stoppage of the previous flow of feelings, images, and insights. Some key questions help, such as, "What is this frustrating sensation, or this 'stuckness,' saying to you? What additional questions do you need to ask yourself? What needs to happen to achieve the desired 'felt shift' and the resulting release of tension?'' The standard progress in this focusing method is the feeling of rightness about the emerging solution and the reduction of tension.

At this later stage of focusing there is the principle of "distancing" to consider. This is an effort to emotionally disengage somewhat to avoid being overwhelmed by the problem or the emotional consequences. Distancing also may help the stuck condition. Another result of proper distancing is that the person is more likely to experience the whole problem and acquire some immunity against strong feelings of anxiety. Again, words and images are encouraged in order to experience the full range of the problem. Several cycles of this process may be necessary to develop a clear approach to the problem and its resolution. One problem in using this focusing method is the strong tendency to revert to cognitive functions as a safety net for dealing with the problem. This is likely when the crucial aboutness experience is slow. Repeating the process when you are more refreshed often facilitates the aboutness experience.

Imagery Mental imagery, or imagination, is another entry method for tapping organismic wisdom and developing possible solutions. I will illustrate a way to use guided imagery that is used commonly by human service professionals. An example is to close your eyes and take a guided tour through meadows and mountains, into caves, and into rooms of bright light—all very rich in symbols that tap organismic experience. After engaging in the rituals and images of the fantasy trip, the person receives a message on a piece of paper offered by an old person. It is asserted that the paper contains an important message. What is it? Often these messages are clear indications for appropriate action. Sometimes they are cryptic and symbolic, requiring more incubation time to experience the full meaning of the projected message. In any case, they are assumed to be messages projecting the wisdom of our experience.

Action As in all methods of problem solving, the final task is to move from awareness to action. Relief from the anxiety of the unresolved problem is usually sufficient motivation to move from awareness, to insight, to intention to change, to commitment, and finally to active solution of the problem.

Application Activity:
Using an Intuitive Problem Solving Style

Choose a problem that you have been working with for some time that involves some decisions, the consequences of which are unknown. It could, for example, be changing your job, moving to another community, attending college, getting married, or having a child. Perhaps you have been thinking of one of these issues, or perhaps you have been thinking about buying a house. You have gone through your checklist of items to consider, and the linear or rational approach suggests going ahead. But it just does not feel right. So, you might try the methods suggested in this chapter, starting with the relaxation response and incubation as a complement to your fact-gathering, checklisting, and rational problem-solving efforts.

NOTES

1 Pearlin, L., and Schooler, C. (1978). The structure of coping. *Journal of Health and Social Behavior, 19*, 2–21.
2 Lazarus, R., and Folkman, S. (1984). *Stress, appraisal, and coping.* New York: Springer.
3 Meichenbaum, D. (1977). *Cognitive behavior modification: An integrative approach.* New York: Plenum Press.
4 Meichenbaum, D. (1985). *Stress innoculation training.* New York: Pergamon Press.
5 Ellis, A. and Bernard, M. E. (Eds.). (1985). *Clinical applications of rational-emotive therapy.* New York: Plenum Press.
6 Beck, A. (1985). *Depression: Clinical, experimental, and theoretical aspects.* New York: Harper & Row.
7 Maddi, S., and Kobassa, S. (1987). Research reported in "Getting Tough." *Psychology Today, 21*, 26–28.
8 Maddi, S., Kobassa, S., and Kahn, S. (1982). Hardiness and health. *Journal of Personality and Social Psychology, 42*, 168–177.
9 Janoff-Bulman, R. (1985). The aftermath of victimization: Rebuilding shattered assumptions. In C. Figley (Ed.), *Trauma and its wake.* New York: Brunner/Mazel.
10 Janoff-Bulman, *Trauma and its wake.*
11 Janoff-Bulman, *Trauma and its wake.*
12 Peck, M. (1978). *The road less traveled.* New York: Simon & Schuster.
13 Jung, C. (1973). *Collected works of C. G. Jung.* Princeton, NJ: Princeton University Press.
14 Mahoney, M. (1979). *Self-change strategies for solving personal problems.* New York: Norton.
15 Thoreson, C., and Mohoney, M. (1974). *Behavioral self-control.* New York: Holt, Rinehart & Winston.
16 Bernhard, Y. (1975). *Self-care.* Millbrae, CA: Celestial Arts.
17 Ewing, D. (1977). Discovering your problem-solving style. *Psychology Today, 11*, 69–73.
18 McKenney, J., and Kenne, P. How managers' minds work. *Harvard Business Review, 52*, 128–136.
19 Mayer, R. (1983). *Thinking, problem solving, and cognition.* New York: Freeman.
20 Dixon, D., and Glover, J. (1984). *Counseling: A problem-solving approach.* New York: Wiley.
21 Adams, J. (1986). *Conceptual blockbusting.* Reading, MA: Addison-Wesley.
22 Adams, J. (1986). *The care and feeding of ideas: A guide to encouraging creativity.* Reading, MA: Addison-Wesley.
23 Bents, M., and Bents, R. (1986). Intuition in decision making. *Journal of Counseling and Human Service Professions, 1*, 48–56.

24 Levy, J. (1985). Right brain, left brain: Fact and fiction. *Psychology Today, 19*, 38–45.
25 Pirsig, R. (1974). *Zen and the art of motorcycle maintenance*. New York: Morrow.
26 Pirsig, R. (1979, December). How to avoid gumption traps. *Family Handman*, pp. 11–14.
27 Russo, J., and Shoemaker, P. (1989). *Decision traps and how to overcome them.* New York: Doubleday.
28 Gendlin, E. (1978). *Focusing*. New York: Everest House.

Chapter Five

Coping with Hassles and Stressors

WHAT IS STRESS AND WHAT ARE ITS EFFECTS?

Because stress is a given in life, the main question is how do we manage our lives to minimize distress and maximize eustress during transitions? The term *eustress* was promoted by Selye, a pioneer stress specialist, to describe the pleasant and stimulating responses to stress. Examples are exercise routines or performing before an audience. Activities leading to eustress usually are voluntary. They serve useful functions in our lives, such as providing the joy of achievement, excitement, novelty, and challenge. Conversely, distress is the reaction to painful and unplanned stressful conditions.

Selye called body reactions to stressful events the "general adaptation syndrome."[1] This means that the automatic physical survival response to powerful stressors is manifested by increased heart rate and endocrine secretions, rapid breathing, contraction of blood vessels, and sweaty palms, resulting in increased alertness and readiness to respond. These physical and mental responses were essential to survival in ancient times, but they often are dysfunctional now because they keep the stressed person in a constant state of arousal.

Eventually this protracted hyperactive state leads to health problems. The following life situations illustrate the need for transitional stress management methods.

Lana recently has become the primary caregiver to her elderly mother. She is caught among the roles of working full-time, caregiving, and maintaining a family. These changes have brought on acute stress responses. So, role conflicts and work overload contribute heavily to a stressed life.

Ted teaches fourth grade, but he was moved to a middle school to teach seventh grade. Although he is accustomed to the satisfaction of seeing immediate results of his fourth-grade teaching, he is disappointed that he does not see more tangible results of his seventh-grade teaching and discipline. He leaves school tense and depressed almost every day. Low immediate rewards contribute to stress reactions because often we do not know if we are successful in the new situation until years later.

Larry recently moved to another job under a demanding and authoritarian supervisor. He constantly feels under strain because of tight deadlines and receiving critical feedback on how he is doing. The new technical changes in office machines are intimidating. Consequently, Larry experiences many feelings of helplessness and powerlessness. He has low support and trust because he knows so few people on his new job. The restrictions of an authoritarian work system add to his stressors. Job stressors are a major source of strain reported in all employee categories.

Hans fears that he is becoming obsolete and that he is not current with the technical and procedural changes in his profession. He experiences constant tension and periodic digestive distress. Hans suspects that his age is becoming a factor in managing the stressors in his profession. Keeping up with technical advances is a major source of stress responses on the job.

These are a small sample of myriad ordinary stressors that people face. Taken singly, these role strains and job pressures usually have low impact, but cumulatively they pack a powerful punch. It is obvious that severe stress is involved with major transitions, such as accidents, disabling illness, and disasters. The stress is so great in these situations that victims usually go into shock or are incapacitated.

Before moving on with the discussion of stress, some definitions are needed. Experts disagree on its definition, but the term *stress* has three basic meanings. It applies to conditions that cause the stress reactions—called *stressors*, or stressful conditions. The results of these external stressors lead to *stress responses*, as described in the foregoing examples. The intensity of the stress response is related to the strength of the stressors opposed by the strength of the person's coping resources. Stress is used in everyday language to mean *strain*—the personal suffering experienced from external or internal stressors. This idea is expressed in the popular phrase, "I'm all stressed out." In this sense, stress is the person's *appraisal* of the persistent effect of stressors.

Effects of Stress on Health

There is growing research among psychologists and physiologists, such as Vitaliano, indicating that coping skills help to alleviate health-destroying stressors.[2] Kobassa and Pucetti's work with executives indicates that their perceived support from superiors was associated with low illness rates.[3] Cousins's work with severely ill people at the University of California: Los Angeles Medical School strongly suggests that certain coping attitudes are especially facilitative in both prevention of and recovery from severe illness. Key protective attitudes uncovered by these studies were hope, positive self-regard, and self-empowerment. These attitudes reduced the subjects' sense of helplessness; hence they also became effective buffers against depression. Cousins has compiled evidence suggesting that growing depression impairs the immune system, leaving people more vulnerable to disease.[4] T-cells, or "killer" cells that protect us from infection, tend to diminish under prolonged stress conditions. The implications of these studies for transitions is that it is important to reduce depressive feelings not only for comfort but also as a protection against illness.

Coping skills for resisting stress also contribute to spiritual health as well as mental and physical health. By spiritual health I mean a sense of purpose and fulfillment that serves to counteract feelings of worthlessness, guilt, meaninglessness, and emptiness that accompany many stressful conditions. Some people feel anxious about the prospect of being happy. They fear that their efforts to be happy will make them unhappy, or that enjoying life will make them feel guilty. This anxiety and guilt could then lead to an endless search for life's meaning. To avoid these feelings we often hurry more and fill our time with busywork. This episodic search for meaning often results in greater sense of strain. When the guilt and frustration from our search for life's meaning overtakes us, our motivation and confidence decline also; we achieve less and experience reduced satisfaction. This stress cycle continues until some kind of physical or mental change brings on a crisis. This crisis then forces us to make some significant changes in our lives to break the vicious circles of distress and efforts at its relief.

Additional mental problems that result from strong stressors are difficulties attending, concentrating, deciding, planning, and remembering. Our judgments are faulty under stressful conditions also, which suggests that we should not make important life decisions, such as remarriage, career change, or moving during stressful transitions.

Types and Levels of Stress Responses

It is useful to distinguish among severe stressors, ordinary situational stressors, and hassles so that we do not trivialize the severe stressors or minimize the hassle effects. For example, June received a ticket for parking illegally after searching at length for a parking space. She also had trouble starting her car, which made her late for work. Taken singly, June's stressors were not great; but the accumulation of responses to such hassles close together put great strain on her coping capacity. According to research by Lazarus and Folkman[5] and by Sethi[6] we usually underestimate the stressful consequences of the small but annoying hassles of life. For many people, the stressful consequences of hassles often are greater than the effects of big changes with which they cope easily.

There are hundreds of change situations that people regard as stressful. *Technostress* is a recently coined term for the strain caused by the introduction of high technology in the workplace.[7] Varied individual styles of responding to stressful situations are related to cultural differences. For example, city driving for a rural resident is often frustrating and fear provoking.

The costs of severe stress responses are high. Examples are proneness to absenteeism, accidents, alcoholism, and illness. Moderate situational stress, especially that stress prompted by a Type A personal response, often leads to chronic distress and unhappiness.[8] Type A personalities, if this is a new term to you, are the hyperactive people who go about their work with a sense of time urgency and intense competitiveness. Recent research on Type A personalities indicates that it is not the hard, sustained work style that is stressful as much as it is the hostility that accompanies the frustrations of slowed and incomplete tasks.[9,10] This hardworking Type A person (as contrasted with the more easy-going Type B) is not the same as the workaholic who works overly hard and long out of a deep psychological need.

Some people, in contrast, experience hypostress (too little). This condition is manifested by boredom, low activity level, and flat emotions known in popular language as the blahs. These people scrupulously avoid conditions or commitments that could be considered stressful. The task for ourselves is to maintain a balance among the conditions that produce excessive stress and put us at risk on the one hand and the tendency to maintain comfortable low-stress and low-risk conditions on the other.

Physical responses to stressors are fairly standard because the body takes normal protective action in case a fight or flight is necessary. Additional behavioral responses usually are evident, such as flushing, explosive speech or laugher, distorted facial expressions, and awkward movements. Mental responses are not as apparent, but they include lapses of memory ("blanking out"), preoccupation with self, and wandering attention.

It is apparent from this discussion that there are great individual differences in tolerance for stressors and meaning attached to stressors. For example, paying income taxes is a stressful event for some people. For others it is a routine, ordinary task that reflects their affluence. Families going through transitions caused by disasters, illness, accidents, and criminal assaults have special problems in helping children attach meaning to that event and to cope with changes in the traumatized family. Figley's *Helping Traumatized Families* would be useful if you face this special coping problem.[11] In addition, painful stressors sometimes produce positive results, such as motivation toward higher achievement and increased alertness to danger. Experiencing a moderate amount of strain before an important examination, for example, serves to keep you alert and clearheaded.

Application Activity: Identifying How You Respond to Stress

What conditions lead to stress responses in yourself? (e.g., deadlines, changes, interruptions, unfinished work, harassment, hassles, and pain). How do you typically respond to these stressful conditions? (e.g., body reactions, unusual thoughts, distressful emotions, and baffling behaviors). What are the vulnerable stress points in your body? (e.g., headaches, chest or stomach pains, weak muscles, tense muscles, sweaty hands, racing or irregular heartbeat, or frequent elimination). I suggest that you make a written list of your answers to these questions for use in the next section.

METHODS FOR MANAGING STRESS

One key to effectiveness in managing your stressors is the condition of your coping skills. Although stress management includes a cluster of special coping skills, the extent of stressor reduction also is a condition of your support system, attitudes about change, problem-solving capacities, thought control, and behavior change methods. The goal of this section is to describe and apply illustrative methods of stress reduction. There are many methods from which to choose; so, if you do not have a favorite and effective method of stress management, you can find one here to suit your life style and interests.

Muscle Relaxation

Physical relaxation is an easy and effective way to manage stress responses. The goal is to be able to relax the large muscle groups with a self-generated verbal signal, "Relax!" Benson called this the "relaxation response," which is based on physical relaxation and meditation effects.[12] Progressive relaxation exercises that lead to this automatic relaxation response are based on Jacobsen's *Progressive Relaxation*.[13] This established professional technique has been adapted for self-administration. There are a number of commercial audio tapes available to help you learn this method, but you can make a start with the following introduction.

Application Activity: Practicing Progressive Relaxation

The first step is to focus attention to the top of your head. Tense the muscles of your scalp. Be aware of this tension in your scalp and now say to yourself, "relax your scalp." This statement may need to be repeated, but you should be aware of a general loosening of scalp and forehead muscles. The rationale for this method is to increase awareness of both muscle tension and muscle relaxation and to experience the contrast between the taut and relaxed muscle. Tightening muscles also helps the muscle to a state of fatigue. A tired muscle cannot stay tense very long.

Then move to the forehead and repeat the exercise—alternatively tensing and relaxing the muscles of your forehead. Do the same for your eyes, telling yourself to squint and then release quickly. Proceed progressively through the neck, arms, fingers, back, legs, and feet. You should be aware in the early stages that return of tension to parts of the body you have covered is likely. If so, repetition with those parts is necessary.

This progressive relaxation routine should take a half hour or less, and it will take less time as you become more skilled. Finally, you will be able just to say to yourself, "relax," and your whole body will go into the relaxation response. It helps to carry out this exercise with a partner exchanging roles in guiding the relaxation progression. The instructions should be given slowly and in a soft voice. Caution is necessary, because this method is also a component of hypnotic induction. Very susceptible people may go into a deep sleep. If that happens, stop the relaxation process. Then you can either let them sleep it off, or simply ask them to wake up. Stay with them until you are assured that they are fully awake.

Autosuggestion

This method may be combined with physical relaxation. It is a method of telling yourself that tension is leaving your body. For example, you tell yourself that "the tension is now flowing out of my body," and you simultaneously visualize this tension reduction. In conjunction with progressive relaxation you can tell yourself that "my whole arm is relaxed; the tension is just flowing away." When finished with your whole body you can say, "my whole body is very relaxed, very relaxed." It helps to repeat this autosuggestion until you are very aware of the reduced tension. If stated softly or in subvocal form, the relaxation response will be enhanced.

Imagery

This is a method of tension reduction through your imagination. Visualize your body in a relaxed state, for example. You can use metaphorical images such as thinking of yourself as a limp wash rag or a bowl of gelatin. You can imagine yourself progressively relaxing as you do the progressive relaxation exercise described previously. To do this you visualize what is happening to your body as you go through the relaxation routines. For example, you see in your imagination that muscle becoming limp.

Another form of imagery is to take a mental trip to a place of relaxation and calmness. Imagine yourself lying on a favorite beach and letting the warm sun and soft breezes caress your body. Associate the image with a relaxed feeling. Similarly, you could take mountain trips where the climbing and scenery are relaxing, or go in your imagination to a concert hall where your favorite music is playing. Close your eyes and imagine going there, sitting down, and listening. Again, associate the pleasant surroundings and events with relaxation. Professional human service workers frequently use more complex guided imagery with their clientele to promote the relaxation response. You can do it for yourself in the simple form I have described. If you wish to investigate this method further, a series of tapes describing and illustrating imagery have been developed by Lazarus.[14]

As a first aid device during a busy and hectic day, I suggest that you look at a favorite scenic picture on the wall. Go to that place in your imagination for a few minutes. You will be surprised how much a short "time out" can refresh and relax you. I keep a large travel poster above my desk showing scenes of Hawaii that create relaxed and pleasant images. I go there for about two minutes during hectic times when the stress responses build up.

One concern about methods that promote relaxation is that they work so well that we often want to sleep, or we resist returning to the stressful realities of the moment. A useful suggestion when you tell yourself to relax is that you will also be alive and alert when you focus back on the task. Thus, the feelings of flowing relaxation will continue, but you will also be alert and attentive to the tasks at hand after the relaxation activity.

Laughter

All of us have experienced feelings of relaxation and well-being after a hearty laugh. A stress management program must include some laughter each day. There are several ways to include some good laughs in ordinary activities at work and at home.

* Look for the absurdities and incongruities in your daily life, and let the chuckles flow freely.
* Associate with people who enjoy a hearty laugh occasionally.
* Develop a collection of stories and real life anecdotes that are humorous and that you enjoy telling.
* Play a funny tape in your car to help reduce the hassles of driving.
* See a funny show, movie, or TV program.
* Do something out of the ordinary for you—like kite flying or sky diving.
* Read funny books and learn to appreciate limericks and humorous poetry.

Humorous situations are difficult to contrive, and humor must be used with care so as not to offend age or ethnic groups. Being alert to the humor in ordinary situations takes a special kind of attention set that can be developed. If you find that these suggestions do not work and that your laughter is infrequent or weak, I suggest that you seek counseling; you may be experiencing a depressive phase in working through your transition. In this phase nothing seems funny, and laughter is absurd or painful. Sometimes others' attempts at humor appear to trivialize your pain. You may need to do what Cousins did to help him through a painful muscle illness. He looked at old movies of Laurel and Hardy, the Marx Brothers, and W. C. Fields on the principle that laughter is good medicine. It worked.

Meditation

Meditation often is confused with contemplation of religious images because it is a part of Eastern religious activity as well as Hebraic–Christian traditions. Meditation does not necessarily have such a connection; it is primarily a method for promoting relaxation. Meditation works best when we shut down our thinking processes and shut out environmental stimuli. Some meditation leaders have commercialized and mystified the process, and huge fees are charged to learn meditation routines, receive personal mantras, and experience the sensations of burning incense. This mystical ritual is not necessary to relaxation and feelings of well-being. The five essential components of meditation can be learned and applied easily. The principal problems are sustaining motivation to continue until the benefits are realized and the obstacles to achieving a deep state of relaxation and well-being are overcome. Meditation includes the following five components:

- Selecting a quiet place.
- Selecting a comfortable sitting position.
- Focusing on breathing.
- Vocalizing a nonsense syllable.
- Practicing the process twice a day.

Meditation should be conducted initially in the same quiet location. After the method is mastered it can be performed anywhere, except while driving a car. It is amazing how extraneous sounds do not intrude after a short time. Meditation can be used to induce the relaxation response in any situation. It could help while waiting for a long traffic light to change to insulate yourself against the tense people around you who are calling on their cellular phones, honking horns, and showing other signs of impatience. I applied the method successfully while in line at a large and busy air terminal that had been closed because of snow. I just shuffled along in the long counter line in a meditative state. I did not pick up the infectious tensions around me, and I arrived at my destination very late, but refreshed and rested.

Posture is important only to the extent that one is in a comfortable upright position with erect spine. Meditation should not be performed while lying in bed, but it helps the process to keep eyes closed to shut out distractions. The idea is not to go to sleep, although meditation can be used for this intended purpose. The goals are to achieve relaxed alertness and a feeling of refreshment. There is also a sense of well-being and tension release in the meditative state.

Mediative states may prepare people for a transformational or transcendent change level. Zen monks, for example, use this method to prepare for desired transcendental change. This is the loftiest possible form of personal change whereby the meaning of one's life becomes more clear and general enlightenment leads to higher levels of consciousness. Meditation is used as a coping method in transitional change only to induce the relaxation response and a consequent feeling of well-being. Meditation can be practiced at any point in the transitional change process described in chapter 1.

Breathing is the essential and powerful component of meditation. You begin by focusing attention on your natural breathing. You say to yourself, "I am aware of my breathing." The rate of breathing usually slows along with appearance of deeper and more regular breaths. You will begin to experience a relaxed state very soon. If this does not happen after a minute or so, you can use the autosuggestion method described earlier and say to yourself, "Your breathing is becoming slower and deeper." This should be a natural breathing process, not forced, because hyperventilation might bring on dizziness and possibly nausea.

Breathing awareness can be used as a first aid method during stressful times at any stage in a transition. When you are faced with a difficult decision or an unpleasant task, such as meeting someone you fear, focusing on your breathing has a calming effect. Performers and public speakers report how much their focus on breathing helps them to feel more calm and confident.

A meaningless *vocalization* during the early stage helps to focus attention and shut out auditory imagery. In the early stages of meditation, ideas tend to flow across awareness and retard relaxation. The resonance created by the syllable as it is repeated helps also. A common example is to vocalize *Om*. Such a syllable is repeated slowly and audibly in the early stages of the meditative process. Specialists in this method call these vocalizations mantras. They assign personal mantras that are unique to a person, but I think this act promotes a mystical quality to the process and is not essential to effective meditation.

Practice and regularity are essential. The usual guideline is to meditate twice a day, morning and evening, for about 10 to 15 minutes in each session. The standard for success is to emerge from the sessions in a relaxed and refreshed state. This condition helps to mobilize motivation and energy to tackle the tasks of the day. In addition, a general feeling of well-being is experienced that usually lasts for several hours. In the throes of a transition, we need all the feelings of well-being that we can generate.

Choosing and Prioritizing Activities

Relaxing activities are limitless because of individual differences, but the fact that time is so finite forces us to choose those activities that are most fulfilling. Sharon, for example, likes to play the electronic organ for relaxation, but she also likes to bowl, golf, sew, paint, and read. She is in constant conflict about which activities to pursue, and she experiences much emotional conflict about how to use her leisure time. Some principles you can use to reduce such conflicts and their stress reactions are as follows:

• Know the strengths of your interests and activities that result in joy and relaxation.
• Prioritize and rank your activities from maximum to minimum relaxation responses, and firmly decide to say "no" sometimes to avoid overload.
• Once decided, stick with your planned relaxation activities long enough to feel good about them and yourself.
• Use your thinking skills described in chapter 4 to give yourself positive messages about your chosen activities.

These statements are not simply elaborations of the obvious from human experience. Activities designed for relaxation do not always result in a relaxation response because many of us have choice conflicts, overplan, or are reluctant to say "no!" Some people have too few interests or they invest their energy exclusively in a cultural, religious, or service activity. This selectivity is a personal choice, and if it serves as a stress reducer, great! Those people who enjoy a wide range of community, employment, and professional activities are the ones who tend to become overcommitted.

There are many reasons for the predicaments resulting from overcommitment. Besides the obvious reason that we like to fulfill certain commitments, we find that doing so enhances our self-esteem. People find that they need us and that we need them. It is fairly easy to plan for a controlled commitment; but then something we really want to do and cannot turn down comes along. So, again we are stressed out from overload. In other words, our personality styles and our ego needs determine to a large extent how we handle choice and commitment issues. If you are unhappy with your present style, it is reassuring to know that it can be changed with determination, effort, and outside help, if necessary.

Planning utilization of your time is not easy because there are so many commitments and priorities to meet. Most of you probably have multiple roles of family member, worker, and community volunteer. You also have your aspirations for relaxing leisure time activities. So, as a person with normal life commitments, you experience much conflict and occasional resentment that "they" are usurping your time. Then, just when you think you have it all together you find that the time commitments were more than you thought, or a life transition intrudes to upset your carefully balanced life plan. Several principles to avoid these time pressure traps are important to remember:

- You control your time; you are responsible for your choices.
- You give permission to allow others to set your priorities.
- Self-knowledge about ego needs, vulnerable points, and personal wishes is essential to plan and prioritize activities effectively.
- A sense of humor to see the absurdities in your life helps you to regain perspective.

Perhaps you remember Pareto's rule from earlier studies. According to this rule, 20% of our activity produces 80% of the results. If this is true for you, then investing 20% of your time more effectively will produce a vastly higher output and probably with fewer hassles and reduced stressors. The stress effects from excessive telephone calls, commuting, meetings, and paper work are within your control. Keep in mind also that the problem is not time management as much as it is self-knowledge and self-management. For example, each of us must know our own tolerance for stressors caused by time pressures, and each of us must take responsibility for managing our own lives. In addition, it is important to realize that our present time management is the result of long accumulation of habits and ingrained personal style. Are you a turtle or a rabbit when it comes to the race of life? Perhaps you are a race horse. Each of us must know our own style and pace ourselves accordingly. The alternative is to go through the demanding process of self-change to amend our styles. If you choose this alternative path to self-improvement, the goal-setting and planning suggestions in this book can be applied.

To change these difficult behaviors takes concentrated and sustained effort. Some critical motivation questions to ask yourself are, "What would the advantage be for me if I managed my time more effectively?" "What would be the consequences of continuing as I am?" "What would I do with that extra hour I would save?"

Because transitions are especially distressing, at times it would help to write the essential tasks that need your attention, such as the next steps in seeking reemployment. This action helps you focus on the essential tasks, reduce emotional confusion, and clarify priorities. Procrastination or protracted "stewing" usually generates additional strain. So make a plan and stick to it. If this caveat sounds onerous or patronizing, keep in mind that time saved means more leisure for your enjoyment and profit. Again, the principle of balance is an important consideration here. You could plan so carefully and manage your time so minutely that you would feel rushed and thus experience even more stress reactions.

Before scheduling too tightly, examine your beliefs about time very critically. Examples of beliefs that cause "time binds" are: "I must work hard and do my best at all times; I must finish my work before I play; I can do anything I set my mind to do; I must always help when asked; It is selfish to take care of myself first; Time is money so I must plan to use every minute wisely." If these beliefs are problems for you, consider the thought-changing methods described in chapter 4. If you want to do more study of time management I suggest you read Lakein's *How to Get Control of Your Time and Your Life.*[15]

Application Activity: Analyzing
Your Time Commitments

Because time management and efforts to prioritize work, love, and leisure activities are the big issues in every person's life, it is a good idea for all of us to go through the following activity on a regular schedule. Doing this activity assumes that you value your time and that you are committed to effective time utilization.

1 Get into a quiet place, close your eyes, and mull over your present life. Have a notebook and pencil handy. Visualize the people, activities (work, love, and leisure), and places. Be alert to images suggested by this survey. After the initial brainstorming and memory harvest, write down your principal commitments in the three simple categories of work, love, and leisure.

2 Make a pie chart from your lists that reflects your present time allocations in percentages of total time available. In addition to the love, work, leisure areas, enter time for activities devoted to life maintenance—sleep, meals, commuting, health maintenance, and service.

3 Go back to your reflective mode and ask yourself the following questions:

• What is most important in my life right now?
• Presently, what do I need most in each activity area (e.g., family caring, alone time for self-development, community service, professional writing, or recreation)?
• How integrated or compartmentalized and fractionated is my life?
• What unwanted obligations have I incurred? Which of these can be eliminated?
• Am I obsessively pursuing any activity to the neglect of others?
• Is a life transition taking place in any area of my allotted time that will affect future allocation of that time (e.g., work change, marital status, or health)?

Make notes of your feelings as you do this reflective activity. How reliable do these feelings appear to be as guides to changing your time allocations?

4 Redraw your pie chart with time allocations that reflect the wishes for change that arise from your reflections. This revised time allocation can now be used to set goals and make immediate and long-range changes.

5 Use the suggestions for setting goals and managing behavior described in chapters 2 and 4 to effect your desired changes. Keep in mind the following suggestions from professional time managers:

- Reorganize your time distribution as suggested in this activity.
- Reduce task time through careful planning and elimination of time wasters.
- Keep in mind that erratic time schedules and chronic tardiness show disregard for others.
- Eliminate unnecessary tasks or low-priority activities.
- Do a task to the finish point, rather than engage in unproductive emotional behavior, and perform those tasks yourself that are most fulfilling.
- Delegate tasks when possible.
- Take regular time-outs in the form of long weekends, vacations, continuing education, and personal renewal to cope more effectively with the unavoidable hassles of everyday life and avoid job burnout.
- Identify your personal strengths and build on them.
- Increase personal efficiency and strive for optimal performance.
- Use aids such as checklists, biorhythm charts, daily plan sheets, or reminder cards to keep your life organized and flowing smoothly.

NOTES

1   Selye, H. (1978). *The stress of life.* New York: McGraw-Hill.
2   Vitaliano, P. (1989). Caregiver stress. *Dimensions,* 4(4), 1–2.
3   Kobassa, S., and Pucetti, M. (1983). Personality and social resources in stress resistance. *Journal of Personality and Social Psychology, 45,* 839–850.
4   Cousins, N. (1989). *Head first: The biology of hope.* New York: Dutton.
5   Lazarus, R., and Folkman, S. (1984). *Stress, appraisal, and coping.* New York: Springer.
6   Sethi, A. (1986). *Stress management of technostress in an information society.* Toronto: Hogrefe.
7   Sethi, *Stress management.*
8   Friedman, M., and Ulmer, D. (1985). *Treating type A behavior and your heart.* New York: Ballantine.
9   Thoreson, C. (1989, August). *Type A personality: An update.* Paper presented at the meeting of the American Psychological Association, New Orleans.
10 Williams, R. (1989). *Trusting heart: Great news about type A behavior.* New York: Times Books.
11 Figley, C. (1989). *Helping traumatized families.* San Francisco: Jossey-Bass.
12 Benson, H. (1975). *The relaxation response.* New York: Avon Books.
13 Jacobsen, E. (1938). *Progressive relaxation* (2nd ed.). Chicago: University of Chicago Press.
14 Lazarus, A. (Speaker). (1982). *Personal enrichment through imagery* (BMA Cassette Recording). New York: Guilford Press.
15 Lakein, A. (1973). *How to get control of your time and your life.* New York: Signet Books.

Chapter Six

Living with Continual Change

The general theme of this book is that we can learn to cope comfortably and effectively with transitional changes. This chapter focuses on coping with illustrative life transitions—both the ordinary and the extraordinary. The main goal is learning how to prevent severe complications from developing out of ordinary transitions. The earlier example of Cousins's personal and professional experience on coping with illness emphasized that our task is to prevent depression and hopelessness from impairing our immune systems.[1] His review of depression and illness studies indicated that depression prolongs illness and that early intervention is necessary to prevent more serious health problems.

CHOOSING A HELPING STRATEGY

People facing life transitions often appear to be muddling along or ignoring the consequences of change. Some ignore the signs that they are entering a transition, such as restlessness, self-doubt, uneasiness, frustration, and impatience. Many people seem to drift through their transitions without apparent focused effort. They depend on rules of thumb or deny that a problem exists. Some blithely assure themselves that everything is alright or that all will come out satisfactorily in the wash. They assume that nature will take its course and that there is little they can do to alter this inevitable chain of events. Another goal of this book is to suggest appropriate strategies for coping such as self-help or professional help, as contrasted with doing nothing or becoming dependent on others.

Self-Help

Self-help consists mainly of reading personal-growth literature and reflecting on needed change. Changes in attitudes and actions then are self-generated. Books can suggest how to change life styles or ease personal problems, but most books suffer from exaggerated claims or suggestions that sound too simple. It is difficult also to separate fact from fiction.

A second source of self-help is the cumulative wisdom of our experience and traditions that are passed through the generations. Examples are parenting and health rules. Although it is prudent to listen to the wisdom of our experience and attend to family traditions, it is also wise to consider the ideas and research findings of behavioral science.

Seeking Advice

Another strategy of avoidance is to ask relatives or friends for advice or to let them offer unsolicited suggestions. Asking for advice could be a wise strategy when expert opinion is indicated, but if it is a pattern or style of dealing with problems it could lead to dependence on others. We then are vulnerable to the power and influence of others. Advice often sounds helpful, but it is usually wrong. Advice is helpful in crisis events when we cannot think clearly, or during the confusing times following separations, imprisonment, unemployment, or financial loss, for example. The most helpful advisers have acknowledged expertise, inspire trust, and leave the final decision on a course of action up to us. In any case, before seeking advice we should assure ourselves that we are not just expressing our dependency and fear.

Professional Help

Once you decide to consult a professional, the main task is to select the best type of help from a wide range of human service providers. Although I focus here on services provided by professional helpers in psychology, health, social work, religion, education, and mental health counseling, I recognize that some people are helped by less mainstream efforts provided by astrologers, channelers, faith healers, folk healers, mystics, and mediums. Strong belief is a powerful healing force. People appear to be healed by a wide variety of practitioner styles and methods—some scientific and some based strictly on strong faith in the power of the practitioner. I suggest that you investigate the person and the practice very thoroughly before you seek help outside yourself. This check can be done through testimonials of others who have used that source, library research on effectiveness of the methods, inquiries into the ethics and claims of the practitioner, and consultations with members of the professional association to which the practitioner belongs.

I would be very leery of people who make extravagant claims about their methods, promise cures, or use exaggerations in the media to tout their services. Reputable helping professionals are quite willing to describe their methods, give cautious estimates of their effectiveness, and provide references on their ethics, competence, and training. Most states in the United States require professional disclosure statements by health and psychological practitioners that outline these conditions of service. There are also consumer protection laws that to some extent regulate professional helping services. Your state or province attorney general's consumer protection division has information on these matters. Local better business bureaus also can be helpful; legitimate practitioners register and must have business licenses to practice for fees.

If the person you are considering for consultation is a physician, nurse practitioner, psychologist, social worker, or mental health counselor, there is a state or province licensing board that regulates practice in those specialties and maintains a registry of practitioners. The following list is a summary of points to consider when choosing a professional service provider to help you through your transition. The practitioner

- describes training in his or her specialty;
- cites experience helping others with your type of problem;
- describes his or her approach to problem solving and style of helping;
- describes the conditions of confidentiality (keeping secrets);
- works in cooperation with your primary care physician;
- informs people about fees, hours, and conditions (such as telephone calls);
- assures you that you are free to terminate the relationship any time; and
- gives information about consumer protection and appeal procedures.

In addition, it is wise to seek out information on the service provider's reputation for results and ethical commitments. After the first visit you should have formed an intuitive judgment about the ease of your working together on your transition issues. In any case, it is important for you to feel confidence in and to have a clear idea of your contract with the helping person.

CHANGES IN JOB AND LIFE ROLES

Job Changes

For most of us, our work is central to our lives. Who we are is defined primarily by our type of work and associates. This is the main reason why unemployment and retirement are so difficult to face. In these transitions we lose an important part of ourselves. Certainly there are financial problems in these transitions, but the psychological impact is far greater, and there are important effects on physical health.

For example, Ted retired completely from his post as minister of a large urban parish. He liked his work of 40 years very much, but declining hearing and vision pushed him toward formal retirement. He quickly went downhill physically and mentally, with frequent respiratory problems, bouts with depression, and decreased motivation for even pleasurable activity. He had done little specific planning for this transition, other than financial arrangements. He is in a very painful transition to an uncertain future.

Laura lost her job suddenly as a result of company down-sizing. She had worked as assistant office manager for 10 years, and this news was a shock to her. She went into a moderate depression and ceased all her social and recreational activity. Laura experienced a variety of physical problems that did not respond to medication. A friend suggested that she see a career counselor, which she finally agreed to do after three weeks of suffering.

Although it is difficult to plan for sudden unemployment, there are some things one can do immediately to ease the pain of such a transition. If reemployment is an immediate goal, then consulting a career counselor who specializes in what has become known as outplacement counseling would be helpful. Some companies provide this service to the separated employee, but you probably will need to fund this investment in yourself. The counselor usually will discuss your current situation; do some assessments of your interests, skills, and experience; and then suggest some career objectives and likely employment options to consider. After this counseling you are largely on your own to seek specific opportunities. Your counselor will help you with skills in this job search phase, if requested.

You may wish to do some assessing and research on your own. A guide to help you along this path is *Outplacement and Inplacement Counseling*.[2] Included are checklists and suggestions for forming your employment plan. There are ideas for your job search, such as networking, writing resumes, and conducting interviews. The goals are to make your job search a challenging problem-solving experience and to keep your hope and optimism high.

Retirement   Retirement is similar to unemployment in psychological impact, except that people have more time to plan and prepare for that last day on the job. Opinion among retirement experts is growing that we should get rid of the idea of "retirement" since the problems of adjustment to not working at something meaningful are so great. Most retirees do some kind of paid or volunteer work part-time after retirement anyway. Nevertheless, retirement is a severe transition for most people, as was illustrated by Ted's retirement. Men appear to have more problems than women because their self-esteem and identity are tied so closely to their work.

Research on retirement transitions suggests two themes: First, the retiree must accept the mixed and often contradictory feelings of relief from job pressures and pleasures of the new freedom on the one hand, and mourning the loss of secure routines and psychological nourishment from the job on the other hand. Retirement must be perceived as a time of reevaluation and entering a new stage of life. The second theme is planning. Successful retirees set the stage in middle age for later changes in their life styles and personalities. They must make plans for financial security and meaningful activities early in life; but they also must plan for psychological changes. Successful copers in retirement realize that the best preparation is to strengthen their personality characteristics of flexibility, helpfulness, intimacy, curiosity, and altruism in their early years to sustain them in their older years. These traits are developed over a lifetime of relationships with people. They cannot be bought or learned out of a book, but they can be improved with focused effort.

In the past, most people planned their own retirement transitions with the help of a seminar on financial and legal aspects of retirement provided by their employer. Now there are courses and specialists who also provide counseling for the psychological adjustments to retirement. Because there are no professional standards for such counselors, the rules outlined earlier for selecting a helping professional apply here, too. Workshops on retirement planning conducted by volunteers under sponsorship of the American Association for Retired Persons are available. There are numerous books for self-help planning also, such as the *Retirement Source Book*.[3]

Becoming a Caregiver

One of the most difficult role changes in life is to be thrust into a caregiver role for an ill family member or friend. Long-term care of an aged or sick relative can be especially stressful because of the special knowledge and the constant attention required. There usually is little hope of relief. Most older and frail adults are cared for by the family and are not placed in institutions. This extensive and demanding caregiver role usually falls to a middle-aged daughter or daughter-in-law. Fortunately, there are sources of help in most communities for chore services, respite care, and home health care. If you need such help, I suggest that you call the Senior Information and Assistance number of your local area agency on aging. For those who can afford special care, there are commercial home services available. In addition, there are professional caremanager services that offer consultation on the kinds of services needed. They also serve as brokers to see that the services are provided. If you wish to do some independent study of the transition to caregiver, I suggest Horne's *Caregiving: Helping an Aged Loved One*[4] or, for a scholarly research approach, Springer and Brubacher's *Family Caregivers and Dependent Elderly*.[5]

MOVING AND TRAVEL

Changing residences can be very traumatic. United States census data indicate that about 20% of families move each year. Moves are traumatic because the familiar cues and faces are gone. The moving loss can be as severe as losing a loved one. As an example, when I was 40 and returned from a professional leave for a year, I became moderately depressed (enough to interfere with my daily living). I also had lived abroad and had just returned from an exhausting speaking tour en route. I attributed the depression to fatigue; but it persisted for three months. Acting as a scientist I began an investigation, including interviews with others who had taken extended leave. I found to my astonishment and relief that most of them experienced depression also, some lasting as long as a year. I cross-checked my data with those at another institution and found similar results. I concluded that the extended change—the travel, living in unusual environments, and removal from familiar surroundings had made me, and others in like circumstances, vulnerable to "transition shock." It was helpful to have this knowledge that the problem is widely shared and has plausible explanations, useful descriptors, and a satisfactory resolution.

Schlossberg's research on families that moved their residences showed that they suffered many adjustment problems, including prolonged depression, which appeared to be due directly to the move.[6] Moving a family is a complex operation. The logistics are horrendous, but moving household effects is simple compared to coping with teenage children who balk at leaving their friends or pets.

Military families moving overseas or returning from tours of duty go through similar transitional culture shock reactions. Changes in jobs, especially if they involve a parallel change of residence, provoke similar reactions. Students who move from high school to college, or from school to job, report varying degrees of this transition shock and its attendant depressive episodes. Traveling—especially for business, but occasionally for pleasure—provokes transition shock reactions also.

The practical question is what can you do about these often severe reactions to common types of life changes? Certainly, knowing the likely consequences of making these moves helps some. At least there will be no surprises, and you can say to yourself, "Here we go again!" Preventive steps in the form of timing the move so it does not overlap with other transition events is helpful. In addition, your conviction about the wisdom of the move keeps self-esteem high—a good buffer against depression and "transition neurosis." This neurosis is a serious condition spawned by fear of leaving a familiar situation and dread about an unknown future. Psychologists label this temporary condition separation anxiety, or what is called homesickness. Positive self-talk and problem solving as described in chapter 4 helps to keep your thinking clear about the move. For example, you could converse with yourself about the joys and opportunities this move would bring. These positive reactions help to offset the effects of adverse expectations and discomfort of the move.

Reading about special issues in preparing for and adjusting to a move helps to ease the pain, prevent conflict, resolve guilt, and keep a marriage from cracking. Holding extensive family councils around the issues of the move keeps everyone informed and offers opportunities to vent feelings. For example, children can discuss their apprehension about leaving friends and making new ones. It would be prudent to attach yourself immediately to support groups in the new community or seek out the local Welcome Wagon if it does not find you. I recommend Raymond and Eliot's book *Grow Your Roots: Anywhere, Anytime*[7] for additional ideas on managing a move; the New York Library Association also has published a useful reading list on moving.[8]

George, for example, was faced with a difficult decision. He was offered a promotion in his company from regional to national sales manager. He had a wife, three children, and a dog. They had lived in their present suburban home for 13 years. George gathered his family around the table after dinner when all were free to discuss the offer and his mixed feelings about it. The family reacted with their feelings and questions. George then sat down with pencil and paper to assess his situation—his needs and desires. He thought about what the move would mean, positively and negatively, for him and the family. He discussed his concerns and plans with his wife, a close friend, and a trusted member of his company. It appeared on balance that the move would be desirable; he then discussed the plan with his family and sought their reactions. This illustration is an oversimplification of a complex and stressful decision-making process, but it points out the need to bring everyone involved aboard early, do a thorough assessment, seek the help of others, and then make a definite decision and plan that the family can live with. After this planning, the process of preparing for the move can take place without so many regrets and anguish about whether or not they made the right decision.

Gloria's job as an advertising executive had lost its allure, and she broke off a dating relationship of two years. She considered joining the Peace Corps. Being single, she had no immediate family commitments to consider, but she expressed much anxiety about such a drastic move. After several weeks of stewing about the decision, Gloria consulted a counselor who specialized in managing transitions. He helped her through a process of clarifying her feelings about quitting her job and her fears of an uncertain future. In addition, they performed an assessment of her strengths and limitations, explored options (including the Peace Corps), and projected various life scenarios and consequences of each. After about three hours of consultations, Gloria decided to delay her Peace Corps plan because the changes she was going through now and those that would be demanded by Peace Corps Service were too great. She decided to work for a year as a freelance advertising consultant to give her time to get her life together. Then she would take another look at future options and possibly decide on another direction.

These vignettes illustrate the two basic options for positive action. George assertively went ahead on his own to plan his career transition. Gloria decided that she would consult a counseling specialist prior to making her final decision. Neither of them chose the common delay and avoidance option that usually turns out to be frustrating and self-defeating in the long run. Both Gloria and George utilized planning, assessing, and decision-making skills to facilitate their transitions.

RELATIONSHIP TRANSITIONS

This category covers a wide range of changes that usually involve crises and are heavily loaded with intense feelings of loss and loneliness. Events such as death, war, separation, abuse, imprisonment, hospitalization, or abandonment exact a heavy emotional toll. Even common events such as children leaving home, toddlers going to preschool, or spouses leaving for business trips can provoke an intense sense of loss. Falling out of love, or being unexpectedly jilted often makes the world seem like it is coming to an end. There is no certain way that one can prepare for these severe losses as can be done in planning a residence or job move. One can only hope that the characteristics of the hardy coper discussed earlier in this book, combined with a strong confidence in one's self, affirmed religious faith, and hope for the future, will sustain one during the transition and through the long healing process. Raphael's *The Anatomy of Bereavement*[9] is a helpful book, especially for helping children through bereavement. Parkes and Weiss's review of the research on bereavement is useful for people interested in the scientific study of dying and bereavement.[10]

One of the complications of losing a close relationship is that other transitions are generated as a consequence. For example, a change of residence often is indicated, social configurations shift, marital status changes if the spouse is lost, and so on. It is very important during these times to keep your life stabilized and the decisions uncomplicated to allow healing to take place. There is plenty of time to plan on the other changes, such as where you will live and what you will do with possessions.

Among these priority decisions is planning solitary time. Time should be planned with people important to you and for allowing them to be comforting and sustaining. Later, attention can be devoted to others affected by the loss, such as children, parents, and friends. Focusing on the concerns and pain of others helps our own healing.

There is no way to express in words what a person experiences during loss of an important relationship. There is no way for another person to understand the painful loneliness and the long tearful nights unless they have been there themselves. The common bond of humanness that goes through all of these experiences is reassuring, but each of us must realize that we go through them alone. The emotional aspects of the loss must be dealt with first through contact with significant other people in our lives. Then the more intellectual things can be done, such as reading about loss and grieving experiences, perusing inspirational and comfort literature, or consulting books such as this one on turning loss experiences into opportunities for personal growth. Reading about the experiences that others have gone through during the same event, such as in Caine's *Widow*,[11] offers some reassurance and comfort.

Usually, grief work with our support network and the healing of time take care of relationship losses. There are groups that can provide help during those painful transition weeks following the loss event. Almost every community has special divorce and widow groups, such as Divorce Lifeline, which are led by people who have been through the experience and can offer the kind of empathy and understanding that are needed. Many churches have such groups as part of their ministry. Larger communities have directories of human services that could identify and help access the type of service needed. There are times when even the strongest person needs professional help, not only in the time of crisis, but especially during those lonely weeks following the loss. Ordinary mourning sometimes turns into severe depression; old quiescent adjustment problems often erupt into an acute stage; bodies rebel by developing a host of ailments.

There are many human service specialists available in larger communities. Few exist, unfortunately, in small towns or rural areas. Some ministers have specialized in grief counseling; some psychologists and clinical social workers have special skills for helping people cope with severe loss; some clinical nurse practitioners and psychiatrists (who are also physicians) have special skills in prescribing supportive medications and facilitating hospital admissions. The problem for most people is that these specialists charge high fees for their time and demand a commitment of time. Grief counseling often is not reimbursable under health insurance policies. Some specialists charge fees on a sliding scale to allow for income differences. If fees are a problem for you, there are low-cost public mental health centers in metropolitan and some rural areas. These sources are staffed by mental health workers from various disciplines. Many social service agencies also have volunteers who specialize in grief counseling.

You should definitely consult with a specialist when you feel your own resources are depleted and you do not know where to turn next. When you are experiencing severe and prolonged depression, disabling physical symptoms, and bizarre thoughts and feelings, or when you are entertaining ideas of suicide, you should definitely seek professional help. There is a wide spectrum of feelings that do not have this crisis quality, but nevertheless are discomforting and annoying. Feeling blue, lonely, guilty, anxious, insecure, incompetent, angry, or lethargic suggests that you would do well to consult with counselors who can help you cope with these ordinary feelings and prevent them from developing into severe and disabling disorders. What you should expect to accomplish with your therapist or counselor is to

- accept the reality and finality of the loss of the relationship,
- experience the pain of grief in the safety of the therapeutic relationship,
- identify and express painful feelings,
- learn to adjust to living without this relationship and to continue living a full life,
- withdraw emotional investment in the deceased or divorced person while keeping the memory, and
- reinvest in new attachments and activities.

Sometimes it helps to consult a counselor even when your life is going reasonably well. You may want to seek this consultation to improve your functioning and capacity for joy, intimacy, and openness. In other words, when you are through the healing process and want to explore your potential for a better life and personal growth or alternative life styles, then consultations with a psychologist would provide this developmental opportunity. It is like seeing your physician when you are not sick but wish to enhance your wellness.

HEALTH TRANSITIONS

There are many health-related conditions that lead to profound life transitions and that severely tax our coping capacities. The most obvious are physical disabilities and terminal illnesses, but lesser known are the effects of disfigurement and physical aging. Adjusting to the loss of mobility, youthful appearance, or specific bodily functions takes time, hardy coping skills, and expert help. Miraculous medical treatments are well known and available through various rehabilitation programs. The more difficult tasks are psychological in nature. Sustaining the motivation to persist in a rehabilitation routine and searching for new training and employment require the help of a skilled rehabilitation counselor. Rehabilitation services are widely available and are funded through several government programs and private health insurance.

Terminal Illness

Although the coping issues associated with disability are complex, at least there is hope of making some kind of satisfying adaptation to life. The plight of the person with a diagnosis of terminal illness, however, poses difficult coping problems. There are the tasks of confirming the diagnosis to understand the probable future course of the illness more clearly and to sustain hope of remission or recovery. The uncertainty of one's longevity and the radical shift of life style and values are issues to be confronted also. Then, there is the task of preparing for the final transition—one's own physical death.

A do-it-yourself approach to sustaining hope, optimism, and courage is suggested by Cousins;[12] Simonton, Simonton, and Creighton;[13] and Kübler-Ross.[14] These readings emphasize the power of positive thinking, use of humor and imagery, and the general principles of psychological healing. These methods supplement, but do not replace, conventional medical treatments; they fill that void between the physical explanation of disease processes and mystical explanations for spontaneous remissions and cures. There are specialists in health psychology who are familiar with these psychological approaches to treatment of severe illness, management of pain, and preparation for death. They should be consulted, especially when your informal support networks or self-help resources are not sufficient.

The possibilities of facilitating a remission or cure of a terminal illness pose a delicate problem. On the one hand, there is abundant psychological and medical opinion that supports placing heavy responsibility on patients for controlling the course of their illnesses. Their focus on hope, diet, imagery, relaxation, relationships, and life-style management, for example, strongly affect the course of the illness. On the other hand, if the expectations for remission or cure are not fulfilled, patients feel guilty or angry that they did not do enough or wonder if they did the right thing. The task is to find that appropriate balance between hope that we can influence the course of our illness and the realization and acceptance of the fact that we cannot control all of the influences on our health all of the time.

For terminal illnesses there are counseling methods that help to ease the pain and prepare for the inevitable final transition of death. Such counseling services are available in many communities through hospice programs. These are special nursing and counseling services for families and patients who are in the final stages of a terminal illness. Most health maintenance organizations have a hospice program as part of their member services. Sometimes they have special resident facilities, but most of the services are provided in the person's home setting. The goals are to promote physical, psychological, and spiritual comfort in the person's last days, and to allow them to die with dignity and in comfort.

Disfigurement

It is a common observation that people who have disabilities or are terminally ill have very compelling needs for coping with their transitions. But the person who has suffered disfigurement through accident, war, or criminal acts faces severe grieving over loss of prized physical features or beauty. Counseling for this transition is essential for maintaining self-esteem, self-acceptance, and a positive approach to life. Psychological counselors can provide an atmosphere of trust in which people can safely explore their fear, hurt, bitterness, and anger. People can gain reassurance about their worth and competence to live a satisfying life with others in spite of their appearance. They also can develop positive plans for a productive life.

Aging

Aging poses special transition problems. Although the loss of vigor, potency, sensory capacity, strength, and youthful appearance usually is slow, it can be rapid enough to strike alarm in the aging person. Our society still has a strong youth bias reflected in the entertainment and advertising media. This age bias contributes to the difficulty that people have in aging gracefully. Many people view aging as a dreaded reality and something to be postponed as long as possible. Increasing awareness of Alzheimer's disease—that devastating condition of slow mental and personality deterioration—accelerates this dread.

Fortunately, there are an increasing number of books—such as those by Brammer, Pratt, and Nolen;[15] LeShan;[16] and Huyck[17]—that emphasize the advantages, joys, and challenges of the aging process.[15] There is increasing research on methods for overcoming the ravages of age such as declining hearing and failing memory. Skinner and Vaughn described ways to enrich our environment to compensate for sensory loss, feel better, and keep our memories sharp through arranging special cues, checklists, and rituals.[18] Counseling with a geropsychologist—a specialist on the problems of aging—could ease the pain of aging, help you accept the inevitable decline, reassure supporting caregivers, and help you replace negative images with positive expectations. The goal is to view aging, in Skinner's words, as "the grandeur and exquisiteness of old age."[19]

ACCIDENTS AND DISASTERS

Accidents and crimes result in especially difficult transitions because they are always sudden and unexpected. Usually, the changes are accompanied by shock and immobility. Accidents and crimes disrupt one's life style and often require a prolonged period of recovery. When the shock of the event subsides it is time to get some psychological help from stress debriefing people or teams to prevent further stress disorders.

In addition to the usual issues of coping with a transition, there are special problems with guilt and anger associated with accidents and criminal acts. Guilt is prominent in accidents because of the "survivor response." For example, you might feel guilty because you survived and others did not. This response is observed commonly at crash sites. Guilt may also be expressed as, "If only I had . . . ". For example, after a car accident the person may indicate that if they had not stopped to see that view, the conditions of the accident would not have been present. He or she feels guilty for having set the conditions for what is perceived as the inevitable accident. Reactions are similar in crimes against people.

Nightmares, sleeplessness, and digestive distress often follow the traumatic event. Self-help for these extremely traumatic transitions is not very likely to be effective in the short run. Consultations with specialists in helping people to cope with traumatic events is essential to recovery. Therapy groups that focus on transitions are especially helpful.

Responses to natural disasters such as hurricanes and earthquakes and human-made events such as train and plane crashes are very similar. Much of what was discussed under accidents applies to these events. The major differences are that disasters involve more people, and the victims usually do not have physical injuries. In addition, disasters involve multiple losses—homes, possessions, jobs, and loved ones. Usually accidents result in financial compensation, whereas disasters rarely result in insurance compensation for the loss of possessions.

It is essential to offer crisis counseling to the victims and families as soon after the event as possible. This stress debriefing helps to stabilize the people emotionally and helps to prevent despair and *posttraumatic stress disorder*, a condition of distorted feelings, physical complaints, and often bizarre thinking or behaving. Stress debriefing individually or in groups consists mainly of encouraging people to talk about the experience and relive many of the strong feelings associated with the event—their anxiety, guilt, and anger. This sharing of feelings has a very healing effect. Then the participants discuss their personal reactions to the event. At this point they often discuss the meaning of the event with some dispassionate analysis. Finally, they make constructive future plans.

A similar stress debriefing program for rescuers, called critical incident stress debriefing aims at helping the medical, police, and fire disaster workers cope with the often overwhelming emotional strain of their rescue experiences. Within a few hours of their experience, the workers are put in volunteer groups under the leadership of a skilled mental health professional. As with victims, these workers describe their experiences and their emotional reactions to them. The aim is to prevent serious mental and physical symptoms when the emotions are controlled over a long period, and to take the burden from family members who often suffer from the irritability and anxiety of workers who bring their unexpressed feelings home.

RENEWAL AND GROWTH

This brief section is an extension of the discussion in chapter 2 on renewal. It is a fitting and positive close to this book on life transitions. When the healing is almost complete and your life has been fairly stabilized, it is time to look to the future with hope and to make optimistic plans. It is time to ask, "What is next for me? What changes in my life style, attitudes, and skills are necessary to get what I want out of my life?" It is also time to set your sights on the stars, to realize your "magnificent obsession," and to look for greater life enrichment. For example, it is time to ask, "What new goals and activities would energize and motivate me to grow in my capacity for joy, hope, courage, peace of mind, love, and creativity?"

It is a time of renewing values you hold dear; this may be the time to compare people values with money, power, achievement, and prestige values. It is a time to ask yourself whether you may have allowed possessions to take over your life and fill the voids. In other words, has the accumulation of money or things contributed to personal impoverishment rather than life enrichment? Times of transition bring us face to face with these critical questions.

It is time to ask what you can now do for others, and how you can return the gifts you received as you worked through your transition. For example, are you ready to volunteer with one of the myriad organizations devoted to helping others find their way through the sticky mud and thick forests of their life transitions? Are you ready also to help them look beyond the pain of their loss to the possibilities of a new and perhaps more fulfilling life beyond their transition? For example, Shirley, a department store senior clerk, was divorced at 55. She went through the usual pain of the separation and subsequent transition. Her future appeared bleak, and the mirror reminded her of her aging body. She expected her health to decline also. As she was reflecting on her transition, she said firmly to herself that she was going to change her life and outlook. This intention moved into commitment and then into action. She applied for, and received, a training grant from her company to pursue management studies; she lost some weight and toned up her body through exercise. Shirley volunteered one evening a week in a local women's shelter. She said she felt younger and healthier than ever before and was pleased with her increased energy and capacity for enjoying life. She said that for the first time in a long while she was doing what she wanted to do.

Renewal time is also the appropriate time to ask what the transition means to you now as you look back. What did you learn about change and about yourself? What coping resources will you need for the next life transition that comes along? Will you be ready to help yourself and help others?

Learning to manage life transitions effectively is a combination of skillful self-management, learned coping strategies, and experience. Sometimes we need the help of others in the form of good coaching. Good coaches focus on a few key points. Usually, improvement on these key points improves overall performance. Imagining clearly how you would want to cope with your transition and then acting according to the principles outlined in earlier chapters is another approach. You will be surprised at the effectiveness of your coping and self-healing efforts. You probably will be pleased at how well you will be able to balance faith in your own power to heal and to renew yourself with the realization that life is difficult, full of contradictions, and bristling with challenging problems.

PUTTING IT ALL TOGETHER AND LOOKING TO THE FUTURE

This is a book about personal change for the 1990s. Change in the 21st century probably will be even more rapid than it was in this last decade of the 20th century. The hardy copers of the next century will need more elaborate ways to think about change—to theorize about what is happening to them and to have refined coping skills and attitudes. This thoughtful personal analysis should enable these future residents to see their everyday transitions with a better informed perspective on issues of control of self and external forces, self-empowerment, self-worth, and self-confidence. This book may help you toward making that thoughtful analysis.

During the 1990s and beyond, we will be challenged to move beyond coping and survival toward achievement of a higher quality of life and more zest for living. This book has emphasized the possibility of seeing the positive potentials in and beyond our current transitions. Not all transitions turn out positively, of course, but the potential is there to understand and to profit from our life changes. We have many models from public life who have moved beyond the pain of their transitions to an even better life. To inspire us there is the classic example of athlete Glenn Cunningham who, after horrible burns, turned his crippled body into a championship running machine. The story of contemporary businessman Lee Iacocca, who was dismissed from Ford management and went on to regenerate Chrysler, is well known. I was impressed by movie director Michael Todd who, after a series of failures and bankruptcies, took additional risks and came through with a huge box-office success: *Around the World in Eighty Days*.

There are thousands of lesser known people who have turned their transitions into positive growth experiences. You may be one of these unsung heroes who have transcended the pain and suffering of a severe life transition. It is encouraging to realize that as our self-esteem increases and the meaning of the event becomes more clear, we are able to focus on helping others through their transition problems. They, in turn, will be able to help their associates, and so it goes into a vast multiplier effect. The underlying assumption is that as we learn to cope more effectively with our own personal change we will be in a better position to assist others to manage their transitions with more satisfaction and effectiveness.

The key points I have made in this book are that we can control the changes in our lives to a larger extent than we might have thought possible. Even though we might not be able to control the unplanned transitions themselves, we can learn to control our reactions to them and, most of the time, to turn them into positive outcomes. Even though I have suggested a general process for understanding transitions, it is important to realize that each person reacts in unique ways within that general process. In any case, you are now aware of a way of thinking about transitions in general and your experiences in particular.

You have assessed your reactions to your transition, surveyed your coping resources, and made plans for leaving the transition with an expectation of renewal and greater personal growth. If you have applied the suggestions in the previous chapters, you now have greater awareness of the importance of a support system and more skills in assessing and enhancing your support. You have increased control over your thoughts and have acquired new skills for changing them from self-defeat to confident statements that reflect your growing personal power. Your problem-solving skills are more varied and functional, and you can manage the stressful events in your life with more confidence and effectiveness. You have more confidence that you can manage your life and take responsibility for what happens to you.

If you are still in your transition, you have a broader basis for hope that you will be able to let go, see new possibilities, and take hold of a new life image. If, however, you are continuing in the throes of confusion and suffering, you can remain hopeful that you will be more able to accept and cope with the occasional bad scenario. In any case, you have deeper knowledge of how your transition has affected your life. You also have more information about how you can strengthen your coping capacity and how to plan for a brighter future.

NOTES

1   Cousins, N. (1989). *Head first: The biology of hope*. New York: Dutton.
2   Brammer, L., and Humberger, G. (1982). *Outplacement and inplacement counseling*. Englewood Cliffs, NJ: Prentice-Hall.
3   Woodbine House. (1988). *The retirement source book: Your complete guide to health, leisure, and consumer information*. (Available from Woodbine House, 10400 Connecticut Ave., Dept. A., Kensington, MD 20895).
4   Horne, J. (1985). *Caregiving: Helping an aged loved one*. Washington, DC: American Association of Retired Persons.
5   Springer, D., and Brubacher, T. (1984). *Family caregivers and dependent elderly*. Beverly Hills, CA: Sage.
6   Schlossberg, N. (1984). *Counseling adults in transition*. New York: Springer.
7   Raymond, R., and Eliot, S. (1983). *Grow your own roots: Anywhere, anytime*. New York: Wyden.
8   The New York Library Association. (1980). *Making your move: The relocation bibliography*. New York: Author.
9   Raphael, B. (1982). *The anatomy of bereavement*. New York: Basic Books.
10 Parkes, V., and Weiss, R. (1983). *Recovery from bereavement*. New York: Basic Books.
11 Caine, L. (1974). *Widow*. New York: Morrow.
12 Cousins, *Head first: The biology of hope*.
13 Simonton, C., Simonton, S., and Creighton, J. (1978). *Getting well again*. Los Angeles: Tarcher.
14 Kübler-Ross, E. (1975). *Death: The final stage of growth*. Englewood Cliffs, NJ: Prentice-Hall.

15 Brammer, L., Pratt, M., and Nolen, P. (1982). *The joys and challenges of middle age*. Chicago: Nelson Hall.
16 LeShan, E. (1973). *The wonderful crisis of middle age*. New York: David McKay.
17 Huyck, M. (1974). *Growing older*. Englewood Cliffs, NJ: Prentice-Hall.
18 Skinner, B. F., and Vaughn, M. E. (1983). *Enjoy old age: A program of self-management*. New York: Norton.
19 Skinner and Vaughn, *Enjoy old age*.

Index